Service Change Management

Practitioner's Guide

A comprehensive reference for practices to manage product and service related changes

An Element of the Universal Service Management Body of Knowledge (USMBOK)

Developed by Service Management 101

An Element of the Universal Service Management Body of Knowledge (USMBOK)

A Practitioner's Guide to Service Change Management
Version 2012.02a
ISBN: 978-0-9814691-6-4

Copyright © 2010 Virtual Knowledge Solutions International Incorporated.
All worldwide rights reserved.
Printed in the United States of America, Published by Service Management 101

Warning: You DO NOT have any rights to reprint or resell any part of this document. You also MAY NOT give away, sell or share, totally or partially, the contents herein without prior written permission.

If you obtained this document from anywhere other than servicemanagement.net or an authorized reseller, it means you have a pirated copy.

Help stop intellectual property crime.

No part of this publication shall be reproduced, stored in or introduced into a retrieval system, or transmitted in any form or by any means (electronic, mechanical, photocopying, recording, or otherwise), except as permitted under Sections 107 or 108 of the United States Copyright Act, and without either the prior written permission of the Publisher, or authorization through the appropriate per-copy fee as defined by a prevailing license. Requests for permission should be directed to: info@vksii.dm.

TRADEMARKS & COPYRIGHTS: Service Management 101 (SM101), the SM101 logo, USMBOK, USMBOK logo, Service Management Master, Outside-In Service Management, Lean Service Management, and Service Management Foundation, and related trade dress are trademarks or registered trademarks of Virtual Knowledge Solutions International Incorporated (VKSII) and may not be used without written permission. All other trademarks are the property of their respective owners.

LIMIT OF LIABILITY/DISCLAIMER OF WARRANTY: The publisher and author have used their best efforts in preparing this book. The publisher and author make no representation or warranties with respect to the accuracy or completeness of the contents of this book and specifically disclaim any implied warranties of merchantability or fitness for a particular purpose. No warranty may be created or extended by sales representatives or written sales materials. The accuracy and completeness of the information provided herein and the opinions stated herein are not guaranteed or warranted to produce any particular results and the advice and strategies contained herein may not be suitable for every individual. Neither the publisher nor author shall be liable for any loss of profit or any other commercial damages, including but not limited to special, incidental, consequential, or other damages. All representations or warranties that may be made in any advertising contained in this book are solely the responsibility of the offeror and neither publisher nor author will have any liability in any regard based upon such representations or warranties.

LIMITATIONS ON USE OF THIS GUIDE AND DISCLAIMER

The purpose of this guide is to provide guidance to service management professionals based upon the opinion of the author. Nothing in this guide is intended to create nor does it create any enforceable rights, remedies, entitlements or obligations. The author and publisher reserve their right to change or suspend any or all parts of this guide.

CONTENTS

INTRODUCTION I
    ABOUT THIS BOOK V
    HOW THIS BOOK IS ORGANIZED VI
    TELL US WHAT YOU THINK VII

INTRODUCTION TO CHANGE MANAGEMENT 1
    WHAT IS A CHANGE? 2
        Common Characteristics of a Change 3
        Essential Requirements 5
    WHAT ARE THE PROBLEMS OF MANAGING CHANGES? 6
    RECOGNIZING THE SOURCES OF CHANGE 7
    TYPES OF CHANGE 9
    FACTORS INFLUENCING THE SUCCESS OF A CHANGE 10
        The Adapted ADKAR Cycle 12
    WHAT IS CHANGE MANAGEMENT? 13
    WHAT IS SERVICE CHANGE MANAGEMENT? 15

GOALS AND OBJECTIVES 17
    INTRODUCTION 17

PRINCIPLES AND SCOPE OF OPERATION 19
    PRINCIPLES 19
        Management of Service Changes 20
        Standardization: 24
        Facilities and Resources: 25
    SCOPE OF OPERATION 26
        The Relationship Continuous Improvement and Change Management 27
        The Relationship Between Incident, Problem and Change 28
        The Relationship Between Change and a Project 30
        The Relationship between Change and Release 31

    The Relationship between Change and Configuration 33

ROLES AND RESPONSIBILITIES 35
    INTRODUCTION 35
    ROLES, PERSONS AND ORGANIZATIONS 36
    CHANGE SPONSOR 37
    CHANGE MANAGER 38
    CHANGE COORDINATOR 40
    CHANGE AGENT 43
    SUPPORT SPECIALIST 44
    CONTRACTORS AND VENDORS 45
    ADDITIONAL ORGANIZATION ENTITIES 45
        The Change Management Group 46
        Change Review Board (CRB) 47
        Change Review Board for High Risk (CRB-HR) 48
        The Continuity Response Team 49

LEXICON 51
    INTRODUCTION 51

KEY ARTIFACTS 55
    INTRODUCTION 55
    THE SERVICE CHANGE RECORD 56
    THE UNIQUE IDENTIFICATION SCHEME 57
    MODEL CHANGE 58
    STANDARD, PRE-APPROVED CHANGE 58
    CHANGE QUEUE 59
    CHANGE CATALOG 59
    CHANGE SCHEDULE 60
    WORK ORDER 60
    SCARI CHART 61
    THE SERVICE CHANGE REPORT CATALOG ITEMS 62

CONCEPTS AND METHODS 63
INTRODUCTION 63
THE CHANGE EQUATION 64
CHANGE LIFECYCLE 65
THE PROBLEM-CHANGE CYCLE 68
ZONES OF RISK 69
CHANGE SLOT 71
THE COST OF CHANGE (CoC) 71

INPUTS 73
INTRODUCTION 73

OUTPUTS 75
INTRODUCTION 75

MAJOR ACTIVITIES 77
INTRODUCTION 77
Assess Phase 78
Commit Phase 78
Apply Phase 78
End Phase 78
HOW TO INTERPRET THE MAJOR ACTIVITY INFORMATION 80
THE INITIATE ACTIVITY 81
Objectives 81
Type 82
Key Inputs 82
Major Influences 83
Related Activities 83
Actors: 84
Key Outputs 84
THE CLASSIFY ACTIVITY 85
Objectives 85
Type 86
Key Inputs 86
Major Influences 86
Related Activities 86
Actors: 87

    Key Outputs 87
THE PRIORITIZE ACTIVITY 88
    Objectives 88
    Type 89
    Key Inputs 89
    Major Influences 89
    Related Activities 90
    Actors: 90
    Key Outputs 90
THE ASSESS RISK ACTIVITY 91
    Objectives 91
    Type 92
    Key Inputs 92
    Major Influences 92
    Related Activities 93
    Actors: 93
    Key Outputs 93
THE CATEGORIZE ACTIVITY 94
    Objectives 94
    Type 95
    Key Inputs 95
    Major Influences 95
    Related Activities 96
    Actors: 96
    Key Outputs 96
THE APPROVE ACTIVITY 97
    Objectives 97
    Type 98
    Key Inputs 98
    Major Influences 98
    Related Activities 99
    Actors: 99
    Key Outputs 99
THE RESOURCE ACTIVITY 100
    Objectives 100
    Type 101
    Key Inputs 101

Major Influences	101
Related Activities	102
Actors:	102
Key Outputs	103
THE SCHEDULE ACTIVITY	**104**
Objectives	104
Type	105
Key Inputs	105
Major Influences	105
Related Activities	106
Actors:	106
Key Outputs	107
THE BUILD ACTIVITY	**108**
Objectives	109
Type	109
Key Inputs	109
Major Influences	110
Related Activities	110
Actors:	111
Key Outputs	111
THE TEST ACTIVITY	**112**
Objectives	112
Type	113
Key Inputs	113
Major Influences	114
Related Activities	114
Actors:	115
Key Outputs	115
THE IMPLEMENT ACTIVITY	**116**
Objectives	116
Type	117
Key Inputs	117
Major Influences	117
Related Activities	118
Actors:	118
Key Outputs	118
THE REVIEW ACTIVITY	**119**

- Objectives 119
- Type 120
- Key Inputs 120
- Major Influences 120
- Related Activities 121
- Actors: 121
- Key Outputs 121

THE COMPLETE (C1) ACTIVITY 122
- Objectives 122
- Type 123
- Key Inputs 123
- Major Influences 123
- Related Activities 124
- Actors: 124
- Key Outputs 124

THE CLOSE (C2) ACTIVITY 125
- Objectives 125
- Type 126
- Key Inputs 126
- Major Influences 126
- Related Activities 126
- Actors: 127
- Key Outputs 127

THE REPORT ACTIVITY 128
- Objectives 128
- Type 129
- Key Inputs 129
- Major Influences 130
- Related Activities 130
- Actors: 131
- Key Outputs 131

KEY PERFORMANCE MEASURES 133

INTRODUCTION 133
- Quantitative (Frequency and Volume) 133
- Qualitative 134
- Financial 135

GOVERNANCE 137
INTRODUCTION 137
THE SCENARIO ACTION PLAN APPROACH 138
The Problem with Policies and Procedures 138
The Scenario Action Plan (SAP) 139
Service Request Pathway 140
Mapping Practitioner Guide Roles to Client Roles 141
The SCARI Concept and Method 142
The SCARI Chart 143
The Major Activity Template 145
Combining Major Activity and SCARI Charts 146

SERVICE MANAGEMENT 101 SERVICES 147
SERVICE MANAGEMENT BODY OF KNOWLEDGE™ (SMBOK) 147
SERVICE MANAGEMENT UNIVERSITY™ 147
OUTSIDE-IN SERVICE MANAGEMENT™ 147
LEAN SERVICE MANAGEMENT™ 147
VIRTUAL SERVICE MANAGER™ 147

This page left intentionally blank.

LIST OF FIGURES

Figure 1: Change Transition State 2
Figure 2: Types of Change 9
Figure 3: Factors Influencing Change Success 10
Figure 4: The Adapted ADKAR Cycle 12
Figure 5: Continuous Improvement Cycle 27
Figure 6: The Incident, Problem, and Change Lifecycle 28
Figure 7: The Relationship Between Change and Release 31
Figure 8: The Release Management 'PUSH', 'PULL' Methods 32
Figure 9: The Change Equation 64
Figure 10: The Change Lifecycle 65
Figure 11: The Problem-Change Cycle 68
Figure 12: Zones of Risk 69
Figure 13: The Change Slot 71
Figure 14: Major Activities 77
Figure 15: Major Activities - 'Yellow Stripe' 79
Figure 16: The Initiate Activity 81
Figure 17: The Classify Activity 85
Figure 18: The Prioritize Activity 88
Figure 19: The Assess Risk Activity 91
Figure 20: The Categorize Activity 94
Figure 21: The Approve Activity 97
Figure 22: The Resource Activity 100
Figure 23: The Schedule Activity 104
Figure 24: The Build Activity 108
Figure 25: The Test Activity 112
Figure 26: The Implement Activity 116
Figure 27: The Review Activity 119

Figure 28: The Complete Activity 122
Figure 29: The Close Activity 125
Figure 30: The Report Activity 128
Figure 31: The Scenario Action Plan 140
Figure 32: The Simple SCARI Chart 143
Figure 33: The Major Activity Template 145
Figure 34: Mapping SCARI Roles to Major Activities 146

Introduction

Change is inevitable, but it's no longer a constant, at least when speaking about the speed and rate at which its happening. We live in a time where change at the personal level is happening at an ever-increasing speed, propelled by faster more mobile communications, technology advancements and simpler acquisition of knowledge.

In the workplace, we face constant change, ever-advancing technologies, new policies and procedures, staff turnover, new customers and opportunities for business growth, reorganizations, shifting duties and reporting responsibilities. These factors and inter-connectivity of today's business and social societies are driving the 'change imperative'.

The change imperative is simple. As a service provider operating in a service experiential economy we must, with limited resources and challenging economic conditions, both enable change, and limit the risk of interruption or unnecessary additional costs, resulting from poorly managed change.

Learning the patterns and principles of change is a must-do. Managing change and increase our resilience and ability to accept and accelerate change is a necessity for survival and success, and the fundamental reason for adopting a formal, yet agile change management system.

I recall one start-up organization where change was happening at an amazing pace as part of high profile, bottom-line critical series of projects. Most, if not all went unrecorded, and frankly, were unauthorized. Those that followed the established change procedures, felt penalized.

There was no intended malice, but with competing objectives and resource conflicts at play, the organization found it equally impossible to meet the service guarantees they had made to the initial wave of customers. It seemed that a step forward in one area caused two steps to be taken back in another.

Soon, they found themselves losing customers, and gaining a new, unsavory reputation for the quality of the products and services they were offering. An outside observer would add they were spending more time on internal conflict and the past, than they were on discussing customer needs, and where they needed to be.

Their support costs raged, with support staff having to work long hours, to the extent many were camped at a nearby hotel for weeks on end. Staff turnover followed, compounding the number, frequency, and duration of issues.

Eventually, the Chief Executive Officer (CEO) issued an ultimatum to all staff. Many complained about the onerous change management procedures. A new Change Manager was appointed. Little changed, except for increased heat in discussions.

The new Change Manager decided to abandon the change procedures that everyone complained of, and replace them with a single sheet of paper. On the paper he had typed one sentence, and a space for a signature, title, and the date.

The paper read:

> **"I hereby assume all risk for what I am about to do".**

The reaction was as you might expect, few were prepared, or even allowed to sign the paper. It was clear most if not all believed the role of the Change Manager was to assume all risk. The Change Manager sent an email to the CEO outlining the situation and suggesting a considerable pay rise, so the salary and benefits could come into line with the level of responsibility this implied.

The issues continued. The change manager emphasized to the CEO that it was not a case of too much change management, or even too little. It was more a case that individuals were not prepared, or unable to be held accountable for the changes they were requesting, sponsoring, and implementing.

The CEO was encouraged to observe proceedings at the next change review meeting. As the meeting began those in attendance were surprised to hear the CEO plan to attend. They were even more surprised to see the CEO enter with a birthday cake topped with numerous lit candles.

"Happy risk day everyone", the CEO shouted. The CEO went on to explain the cake, and how it represented the entire risk of any single change. "The responsibility of the change manager is to share out the risk represented by this cake, fairly, and based upon the proportion of risk each of you introduce by your role in sponsoring and implementing the change.

The CEO continued, "Assume the change manager does not like cake. Assume that all, of this cake is to be shared among those involved in the change. My understanding of the change manager's role is to develop the simplest procedures to help you all understand and accept the size of your share. Oh one last thing, you can also assume any cake left over will be returned to me in my office."

This visual was the beginning of a transformation in how staff regarded changes, change management procedures, and the role of change manager. This was reinforced by the dictate to the change manager to create a new set of procedures that were flexible in their use, matching the levels of checks and balances with the degree of risk. The change procedure had to be proportional to the risk in each change.

In return, the change manager asked, and received, the followings statement from the CEO for inclusion in the new change procedures manual:

"It is imperative we can accept change at an ever increasing pace and known risk. Our change management procedures exist to enable change and to identify and allocate the risk.

These procedures have the strong endorsement of the entire executive management organization and must strictly followed for every change.

Adherence to these procedures not only helps to maintain an effective and efficient functional service and system environment, but it also ensures that this environment is secure and expandable to new technology, customers, and software programs, and that our business succeeds.

All changes to the production environment are subject to these procedures. All personnel are responsible for fully familiarizing with the contents of this document. Failure to comply with these procedures will result in instant dismissal, **followed** *by the arbitration process."*

It worked.

The core goal of the Guide Universal Service Management Body of Knowledge (USMBOK) publication, is to respect all sources of concepts and methods, and to produce a common, universally set, applicable across all service industries and organizations.

As an authorized companion and extension, this reference presents to you a universal set of practices, concepts and methods to manage changes, related to the offer, fulfillment, provision and support of services.

The information in this reference is augmented and complimented by "do and don't" guidance accessible online through the Service Management Body of Knowledge (SMBOK) subscription service. More information in the form of video tutorials about the SMBOK service is available at the SMBOK website:

http://www.smbok.com/pages/smbok-tutorial-home

Thank you for your interest in this book.

Ian M. Clayton
Principal, Service Management 101, Certified Service Management Professional

About this Book

This book is intended to provide a comprehensive description, a specification, and act as a practitioner's guide for service management professionals developing practices to manage changes as they relate to products and services.

This book is a companion and authorized extension to the Guide to the Universal Service Management Body of Knowledge (USMBOK) publication, and provides a detailed description of the USM650 Service Change Management knowledge area.

As a guide for practitioners this book draws upon generally available terms, methods, concepts, and guidance used across all industries regardless of sector. Its development started with a universal perspective and inclusion of all theory and concepts regardless of their source.

It is also designed to be compatible with relevant international standards, such as ©ISO 20000-1:2011 and ISO 9001, popular best practice frameworks such as the IT Infrastructure Library (ITIL®), COBIT®, and proven change management practices used to manage individual and organizational change.

How This Book is Organized

As a practitioner guide this book was produced with you and your needs as a service professional in mind, and the overriding goal to put into your hands a reference makes the management of changes as they relate to products and services, understandable and usable.

The book is a reference book and organized so you can flip right to what you need, when you need it.

This book is formatted to be consistent and compatible with the topics discussed in the USMBOK, and as used to present both education delivered through the online Service Management University, and the online Service Management Best Practice Statement Library. The topics include:

- An introduction to the universal perspective and knowledge area;
- Goals and objectives;
- Principles and scope of operation;
- Roles and responsibilities;
- Key benefits and problems;
- A lexicon of key terms;
- Key artifacts, concepts and methods;
- Major activities;
- Key performance measures;
- Governance;
- Bonus material on scenario action plans.

The sequence of topics is also designed to unfold for you in an easy to digest, incremental manner, and act as a source for the development of custom standard operating procedures.

Tell Us What You Think

Your feedback on this book will help us make quality improvements to upcoming editions and the companion online services. There are a number of methods to provide this important feedback:

1. By entering your comment, suggestion or idea at our support site here: http://www.sm101-support.com/ideas.php
2. By completing the form on this page and emailing it to us at: info@servicemanagement101.com

Feel free to copy and distribute this page to others on your colleagues. For example, what changes would help you most? Please check as many as you wish.

	Your Selections
☐	Add more diagrams to support commentary
☐	Add more information about adapting the information into personal needs
☐	Expand information in areas necessary to apply the subject matter
☐	Improve clarity and consistency of writing style
☐	Improve organization of information
☐	Improve technical accuracy of information
☐	Make information easier to locate using the table of contents, or index
☐	Target the reader more appropriately
☐	Improve the references to specific topics within this publication
☐	Other – please specify in your comments below

Please use this space for any additional comments or suggestions you may have:

Please identify yourself so we can contact you directly if we have any questions about your remarks:

Your Name:		Organization:	
Email:		Phone Number:	

This page left intentionally blank.

Introduction to Change Management

There is an underpinning theory that change happens at the individual, organizational, societal, and infrastructure level. Although it's practically impossible to anticipate when, where, and how change will happen, we know we need to plan for it.

Change is inevitable, necessary, and risk laden. Change is almost always disruptive, yet essential for progress. Those who know how to anticipate it, assess the inherent risk, and manage it, will be more successful than those who don't.

If the reasons for change are unclear or unknown, and the risks unshared, social, human, and organizational friction can manifest itself as resistance to the change.

Every organization must be able to change to pursue new opportunities for growth, and it is key they are able to manage the synchronization of their systems, methods, staff and organization with the required speed of change needed for survival and success.

For change to be accepted, for change to be discussed, for change to form a strategic part of a transformation or improvement initiative, it is important there is a common understanding among all audiences of what represents a 'change'.

It follows that changes need to be accompanied by information, policies and procedures designed to help everyone involved and affected by a change to adapt.

What is a Change?

What is a *'change'*? As can be read in the following simple examples, the use of the term 'change' can have a wide range of consequences and meanings depending on the context:

- "They had a change of mind";
- "There was a change of governance";
- "The policy has changed";
- "We have changed equipment";
- "There has been a change of location";
- "The operating procedure has changed".

Obviously, its common to speak to what has changed. In a products and services context, any of the above examples may be true of a change, and we can only speculate as to why something changed, or the actions that took place behind the scenes to implement the change.

It is important to note that despite the common belief the primary cause of change is to address a problem; the most popular reason for change is opportunity. The process of changing always provides an opportunity to improve, even after a problem.

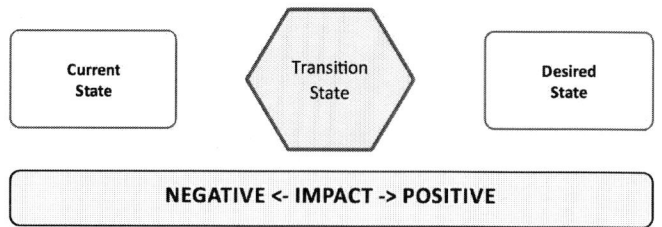

Figure 1: Change Transition State

One universal cross-industry understanding of the term 'change', is that it represents a transition from a current known state, (sometimes referred to as the status quo), to a new, desired and specified state, (sometimes referred to as the future state).

Common Characteristics of a Change

Regardless of industry, a change has common characteristics that influence the procedures designed to invoke a suitable response. These include:

- They result from problems or opportunities to improve;
- They have a sponsor;
- They have a positive or negative effect (impact) on one or more entities and stakeholders;
- They may impact entities other than the sponsor;
- Their scope of impact may be limited to, or include all of, the following:
    - You-change – affecting a person ('you'), or individual infrastructure items;
    - We-change – affecting a group ('we, us'), or an infrastructure domain;
    - All-change – affecting the organization ('everyone'), or the entire infrastructure;
- They have a type implying the reason or cause for the change;
- They require resources to plan and implement, and often this involves cross-function or team collaboration;
- They may interfere, depend upon, or interact with other changes and require careful scheduling to ensure or avoid this;
- The may require careful scheduling to ensure the correct resources are available;
- They have a target time by which they need to be completed and a period of time during to complete the implementation;
- Apart from information regarding other changes they rely completely upon input from external sources- external to any change management system;
- Without proper communication and information they can raise barriers, resistance to change;
- They include a level of risk;
- They incur a cost to complete, often initially unknown and non-budgeted;
- They result in an individual or organizational learning experience.

With respect to the initiation, approval and management to completion of a change:

- There can be a difference across the provider organization, and even within the customer community, of the definition of what constitutes a change, and a lack of reliable information about the reason for a change and its impact when it occurs;
- Every change is a potential disaster, in every sense of the word, including the goals of all involved, loss of assets, reputation, and satisfaction levels;
- There can be unclear or unspecified objectives, sometimes selfish in nature and promoting the interests of the sponsor;
- The change agents can have differing organizational structures and governance procedures for decision making;
- There can be a lack of team structure for coordinated planning between responsibilities;
- Lines of authority may be unclear, with inappropriate or inefficient supervisory and reporting structures;
- There may be terminology differences between all involved and a lack of common terms;
- No effective or functional centralized change control system – those involved may operate on the luck and personality of its leaders. In some situations, the operational effectiveness can depend on which leader or supervisor was working that day;
- Insufficient methods for assigning resources effectively, little or no method for inter-organization allocation;
- A change request consumes resources, and therefore incurs a cost, most likely unbudgeted;
- Whether, and how a change is implemented, can seriously affect the overall satisfaction, and thereby loyalty, and relationship, a customer has with the service provider.

A change represents an opportunity to improve. It is an investment in doing the right things, the right way.

Essential Requirements

These and similar characteristics have caused a number of essential requirements to become clear:

- A systematic method or 'system' is required to enable, initiate, assess the risk, and implement changes in a controlled, cost effective and timely manner;
- The system must be organizationally flexible to meet the needs of change of any kind and size;
- The system must be able to be used on a day-to-day basis for routine situations as well for those requiring a specialized and expansive response, such as major emergencies, and be compatible with the methods and language used by third-parties, such as public and government agencies, who may be involved in the response;
- The system must be sufficiently standard to allow personnel from a variety of organizations and diverse geographic locations to rapidly meld into a common change management structure;
- The system must be cost effective, and include suitable governance, protocols, policies and procedures to authorize the allocation and use of resources, and overall response;
- The system must allow for the planning of a response prior to the event occurring, and support scenario based testing and practice;
- The system should collect, aggregate and generate information in support of a commitment to continuous improvement the effectiveness and efficiency of how changes are managed, and improvements made.

The management of changes requires a formal set of procedures authorized by senior management, and socialized across the entire provider organization. The task of designing a standardized management system should form part of an overall service infrastructure management responsibility.

What are the problems of managing changes?

The management of changes invites a number of challenges for organizations and the individuals involved. Common problems with managing changes include:

- An inconsistent definition of what represents a change;
- A lack of reliable information about why a change should occur;
- Communication about the need is non-existent, the need is not "obvious";
- Differing opinions about the need for change;
- A change collision occurs, where the items being changed are the same but for different changes, or there is competition for the same time periods, resources, or even pursuit of the same outcomes but using different methods or approach;
- The desired outcomes are incomplete or nor specifically defined in terms understood by all the affected stakeholders;
- The desired outcomes are not communicated properly, although the process may be;
- Parts of the organization may be overlooked for direct or indirect impact;
- A belief by one stakeholder that another stakeholder's goals are contrary to their own, or that the impact to them is undefined, or has not been properly considered;
- The plan to implement the change is sponsor specific and stakeholder agnostic;
- Lack of system or method to monitor issues and identify potential problems;
- Inadequate determination of resource needs;
- Communication is inconsistent, incomplete, and/or not supportive of the change;
- Governance poorly defined, especially sponsorship, stakeholder impact, and the specific responsibilities of the roles involved and 'hand-off';
- Inadequate and incompatible risk assessment and risk assignment methods;

- Failure to integrate changes with:
    - An existing continuous improvement program;
    - An existing problem management practice;
    - An existing release management and facilities management practice area;
    - The service planning function;
    - The service support systems and functional responsibilities;
- Inefficient assignment and monitoring of the work effort;
- Inability to match budgeted effort to cost of change;
- They cause new incidents and problems to occur, sometimes seemingly unrelated.

Recognizing the Sources of Change

Change can come from many directions, from sponsors within the service provider organization, from personal initiative, and as a result of external influences. They include:

- **Changes from within:** representing the most common source of change;
- **Responding to rivals:** often as a result of market research, customer feedback, and general business planning activities such as collateral review;
- **Responding to opportunity**: again perhaps from similar information sources as responding to rivals, but also as a result of increased capability, capacity, perhaps from innovation efforts;
- **Responding to problems:** recognizing and responding to problematic situations that impact a stakeholder sufficiently to encourage a change, and an opportunity to improve;
- **Changing to grow:** enabling normal growth and expansion as a result of mergers and acquisitions;
- **Changing to win:** supporting product management strategies and tactics to differentiate products and services, perhaps through review of win-loss reports;
- **Changing to protect:** stabilization of a successful market position, introducing additional control barriers, policies and procedures designed to ensure the status quo across the board, or in specific areas of the operations and product functionality.

The drivers for change can sometimes be beyond the control of the organization and its individuals, and result from:

- Defects, both 'bought-in', or developed in-house;
- The need to comply with a change in regulations;
- The need to comply with supplier mandates for ongoing maintenance procedures;
- Infrastructure wear and tear or deterioration from use;
- Consumption and the need to replenish consumable elements;
- Upgrades resulting from supplier suggestions or mandates.

To deal effectively and to plan properly for increasing rates of change it is important to understand the underlying cause, these can typically be categorized thus:

- Social: general trends in society, politics and demography influence customer demand;
- Economic: impact driven based upon defined problems and opportunities;
- Technical: the revolution in technology is having a profound impact on methods of management, manufacturing, service, purchasing and use;
- Legal: mandatory federal (national) or state (local) regulations require change.

Change is always incremental, but it can be applied gradually, over a prolonged period at a steady rate. It can be radical, sudden and dramatic, with marked effects and noticeable risks. Or, it can be a result of recovering from, or averting a catastrophe.

Types of Change

There are four types of change, also referred to as 'maintenance', these are:

- *Preventive Maintenance*: Involves a systematic schedule of inspection and the maintenance of service infrastructure in satisfactory operating condition by detecting and correcting likely failures either before they occur or before they develop into major defects;
- *Corrective Maintenance*: Modifications made to a service following deployment, to correct failures and discovered problems as they occur. Includes the determination of the cause of a failure and to make corrections and changes to requirements, design, code, test suites, and documentations as necessary;
- *Adaptive Maintenance*: Ensures a service remains usable in a changing environment. Sometimes a change introduced in one part of service environment or infrastructure requires changes to other parts. Adaptive maintenance is the implementation of these secondary changes.

The fourth category, 'perfective maintenance', is a responsibility of the service planning function, and detailed within the service and service revision plans. The four categories are further classified as reactive (post issue) or proactive (pre issue).

	CORRECTION	**ENHANCEMENT**
PROACTIVE	Preventative	Perfective
REACTIVE	Corrective	Adaptive

Figure 2: Types of Change

All 'maintenance' is approved and applied as a result of the change management system. The system should be available to the maintainer with a suitable level of access to allow proper planning and scheduling and the avoidance of issues caused by, or to take advantage of less disruption resulting from simultaneous maintenance required to related service elements.

Factors Influencing the Success of a Change

There are a number of factors to take into consideration when determining the likely success of a change.

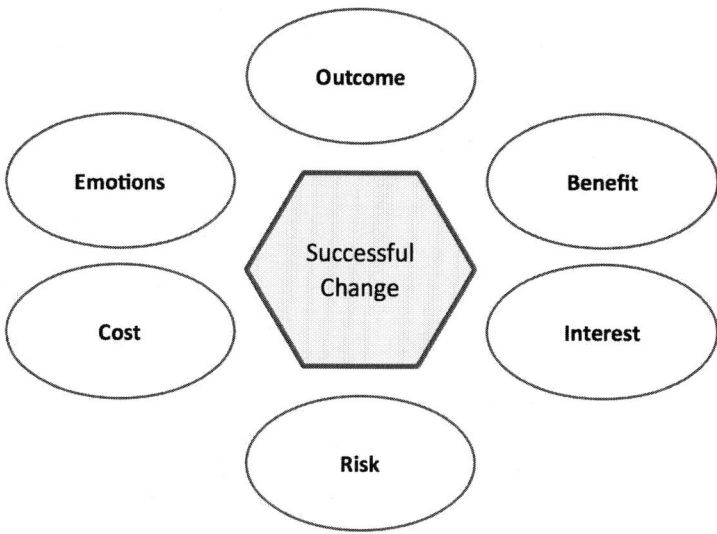

Figure 3: Factors Influencing Change Success

Outcomes: the availability of a clear statement of the desired outcome of the change, presented in terms understood by each stakeholder, especially those directly affected, or who you wish to sponsor or advocate.

Benefit: similarly, it is important the benefit is succinctly stated, again in the terms of those stakeholders directly affected, and personalized where possible by linking it to specific objectives and targets they know of, and are responsible for.

Interest: a description of the interest of each stakeholder regardless of whether they are directly affected by the change. This is important when mobilizing influence, authority and gaining approval for the change.

Risk: the extent to which the technical, business and personal risks associated with implementing, and not implementing the change, are described and accepted as accurate or reasonable.

Cost: access to an estimate of the actual cost of implementing the change, sanctioned by financial subject matter experts, for comparison with the descriptions of the outcome and benefit.

Emotions: recognizing that emotions play a powerful part in decision making, and ensuring the manner in which the change is presented, and the timing involved, enables people and culture to adapt.

A successful change may well have to rely heavily on a problem management function, skilled in the definition of a problem, an opportunity, and the impact or effect of a change.

It may also rely on the organization's ability to apply organizational change management thinking to those changes that directly impact culture, reward systems, and similar motivational levers.

The Adapted ADKAR Cycle

There are a number of factors that will influence the eventual success of a change. In his book "How to Implement Successful Change in Our Personal Lives and Professional Careers", Jeffrey M. Hiatt offers a framework for diagnosing why some changes fail while others succeed. The model is named 'ADKAR', after the five building blocks to success:

- **AWARENESS:** of the need for the change;
- **DESIRE:** to support and participate in the change;
- **KNOWLEDGE:** of how the change will be implemented;
- **ABILITY:** to implement required skills and behaviors;
- **REINFORCEMENT:** to sustain the change.

The following diagram has been adapted from the 'awareness-desire-knowledge-ability-reinforcement (ADKAR)' model[1] to describe factors influencing success.

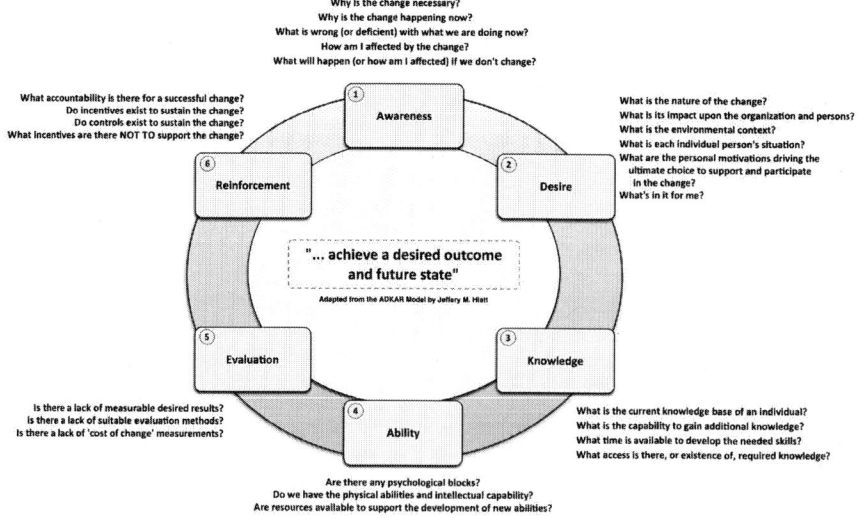

Figure 4: The Adapted ADKAR Cycle

In the diagram, the ADKAR model has been adapted with additional questions and an additional building block – 'EVALUATION', to bring it more into line with current change management systems thinking.

---

[1] How to implement successful change in our personal lives and professional careers, Jeffrey M. Hiatt, 2006

What is Change Management?

Change Management represents an orderly, systematic approach to the planning, communicating, documenting, coordinating, scheduling, monitoring, and controlling of changes. It protects the environment from changes that are potentially disruptive, or have an unacceptable level of risk associated with them by ensuring a change is prepared properly, subject to inspected, and approved by appropriate levels of staff.

Change management methods exist to enable and accelerate the speed of change, and to provide the operational capability needed to ensure standardized methods and procedures are used for efficient and prompt handling of all changes.

Change management methods provide a consistent, flexible and adjustable organizational framework within which entities at all levels can work together to manage changes, regardless of their origin, outcome, resource burden or complexity, and to ensure appropriate levels of authority are involved in assessing the risk and approving the progression of the change.

Change management consists of a core set of doctrines, concepts, principles, terminology, organizational protocols, methods and skills, to provide a consistent framework of actions and governance to manage a change through its entire lifecycle, from initiation to implementation. It is the governance used to transform an organization and its constituent parts from their current state, to a desired and improved new future state.

A service provider organization is required to operate a specific change and maintenance management system dedicated to the responsibility of recording, scheduling and reporting on required maintenance.

Change management *'unfreezes'* the organization and infrastructure to prepare it for change. Providing feedback to the organization members on their attitudes and behaviors, using techniques such as education, participatory decision-making, and command to promote the need for change, and avoid having to impose changes on stakeholders.

Change management *'refreezes'* the organization and helps stakeholders and actors adapt to their new roles and the changed system by providing positive feedback on their changed attitudes and behaviors.

Refreezing activities also make it more difficult for stakeholders to revert to their old attitude and actions and behavioral patterns. Change management provides a basis for:

- Recording reasons for, and details of a change;
- Weighing the risk, cost and benefit;
- Defining and checking for desired results;
- Facilitating more change, faster;
- Knowing when we have succeeded or failed;
- Tracking improvement and preparing for the next change.

Change management provides management with accurate information on the rate and type of change, and ensures evidence of change is recorded.

For many, change management is the single most important element or successful business management today, supporting a continuous opportunity to improve and remain competitive in an increasingly aggressive market.

What is Service Change Management?

The Universal Service Management Body of Knowledge (USMBOK) provides an explanation of a service, preferring a definition found in legal circles, as follows:

"A service is any act or performance that one person can offer to another that is essentially intangible and does not result in any transfer of ownership. The value of the service to the customer is through the results achieved through its use – the outcome. The importance of the service to the provider is through the satisfaction and value it provides the customer, the revenue it generates for the provider, versus the cost of production. Its distribution and use may be tied to a physical product."

As the legal definition states, a service is generally described as work performed by one group that benefits another. The USMBOK defines a 'service change' as, *"The activity of altering the state of a resource known to be required to provide a service, from its current known state to a different, specified desired state. This is normally associated with adding, moving, removing, or modifying a service component or configuration item, with prior approval."*

This can involve a change to documentation of any kind, the organization, hardware and software, policies and procedures, performance reward schemes, staff responsibilities and activities, and so on. Any element, any item deemed necessary to satisfy customers by delivering the service as promised.

Service change management is a specialized adaptation of universally applicable change management methods, designed to provide a systematic method to manage changes as they relate to services, their infrastructure, service guarantees, and the vital mission activities performed by users and customers of a service.

Service changes are progressed through their lifecycle based upon specific criteria and priorities agreed within service contracts or agreements. The activities of moving a service change through its lifecycle include:

- The initiation of a change request, and matching of sponsorship and advocates;
- The creation of a plan to implement the change;
- The classification of the change based upon its relationship to the services, communities, and service infrastructure, and stakeholders in general;
- The setting of the priority based upon its impact, urgency, and the situation level;
- The assessment and documentation of the risks involved;

- The assignment of a categorization, indicating the level of authority and governance required for further progression;
- The approval of the change;
- The allocation of resources to progress the change;
- The scheduling of the change in the service and work calendar;
- The building and distribution of work orders and coordination of the work orders as they relate to the change plan;
- The testing and quality assurance of all aspects of the change;
- The implementation of the change by completion of the assigned work orders;
- A review of the completed change to verify the desired results have been achieved, and completion and closure of the work orders and change record.

Service changes are managed through their natural lifecycle in the context of the service commitments made. Service changes management represents the need to address problems, and continuously improve, while continuously ensuring service commitments are met, and customer satisfaction levels maintained.

Goals and Objectives

Introduction

The primary goal of service change management is to enable, initiate and coordinate the implementation and completion of changes to the service infrastructure in a risk-assessed, cost effective, and timely manner. Other service change management objectives include:

- To provide a systematic approach to the implementation of changes to the approved service infrastructure environment and ensure changes are valid by relating them to a sponsor, cause, source, problem, an opportunity, or new requirement;
- To eliminate unauthorized, and avoid uncontrolled or undocumented changes;
- To minimize the risk of failed, or bad changes that interrupt or degrade service levels;
- To minimize consequential incidents, service impacts, unplanned downtime and longer resolution times resulting from ineffective and inefficient change management procedures;
- To design change management procedures that are compatible and proportional to the scenario context of a change request, and to increase the organization's ability to absorb high levels of change;
- To ensure changes are implemented within the performance criteria described in service contracts as service level guarantees;
- To ensure changes are managed and completed to in a manner compatible with emergency preparedness, major incident, and continuity plans;
- To ensure all changes are in compliance with any organizational mandates, or government regulations;
- To provide methods for assessing and documenting the risk of change, and to ensure each change is risk assessed, and to describe the beneficial impact and risk of change to using language and terms understood by stakeholders;

- To maintain a calendar of changes completed in the recent past, currently active, and scheduled in the immediate future;
- To detail the actions, resources and work effort sequence required, and used, to implement a change;
- To authorize and allocate resources to make changes and ensure efficient and effective performance of change management activities;
- To coordinate and improve the sequencing and prioritization of change related work order effort, and to direct support resources where required;
- To ensure each change is a member of a release unit;
- To progress changes in a timely manner with minimized unnecessary impact to stakeholder activities and work order participants;
- To ensure a complete and accurate record of each change and their journey through the lifecycle, and produce accurate information and reports on change requests to enable the efficient and timely processing of changes
- To create and publish detailed narrative reports that contain the facts, conditions, circumstances, analysis, conclusions and results achieved from implementation of changes;
- To provide information to other service management responsibilities and practice areas to enable their involvement and use of change management procedures;
- To provide a governance method to authorize and allocate resources to implement changes to aspects of other service management practices;
- To promote a better understanding of the value of change management throughout the stakeholder communities.

Principles and Scope of Operation

Principles

Principles establish management direction, mandates, and core themes for the development of guiding documentation such as standard operating procedures (SOPs). Principle statements are designed to aid the decision-making process, and lead to policies and governance to better align the objectives of the service business and service provider organization with those of its business community and customers.

Principles are durable statements about the role of a practice area addressed by SOPs, in this case service change management, and they are:

- Agnostic of product, service, customer, vendor, and technology;
- Representative of best practice guidance at the general operation level;
- Set direction and are actionable;
- Function as a filter during policy decision making;
- Promote consistency in any decision making process;
- Represent the beliefs of the organization and establish a mandate with appropriate sensitivity to the constituents it serves.

In recognizing the following principles, this SOP document is subject to any policies published as part of the prevailing IT Governance Framework (ITGF). The ITGF describes fundamental policy statements about the role of IT and the use of technology in support of customers and the business, and as used to guide strategic level service management decisions.

A set of 'standard' principles should be established by combining the guidance in this publication with other guidance, and the policies within a governance framework, and not deviated from when defining, analyzing and planning the response to a change request.

Management of Service Changes

The roles named in these principles are described in more detail in the 'roles and responsibility' section of this document.

- **Change Record:** A service change should be raised and processed as a separate record – a change record. It can alternatively be recorded as a type of service request under specific conditions;
- **Accurate History:** It is the responsibility of the assigned Change Coordinator to ensure a complete and accurate record is maintained for each change, including a narrative of its journey through the change lifecycle;
- **Scope:** A 'statement of scope' should be written and published by senior executive roles, and by default should include the entire portfolio of services and their related operational and provisioning activities. Any exclusion must be specifically stated and authorized by executive levels of management. This statement should form the charter for any practice;
- **Relaters:** When defined, a change record should be able to be related to supporting evidence, such as an incident or problem record, an opportunity statement in the improvement queue, and other information related to the origin and cause;
- **Project:** Where evident, the relationship to a change and a project must be noted within the change record;
- **Consumer Scenario:** When recorded, a service change should be related to the consumer scenario, consisting of information describing:
    - The activity being performed and affected by the situation;
    - The objective or desired outcome of the activity and consumer (user) performing the activity;
    - The location where the activity is being performed and the user resides;
    - The community to which the consumer belongs;
    - Any infrastructure item (configuration) item known to have an issue, being used to perform the activity, or related to these;
    - The service guarantee most closely related to the activity, consumer, location or service;

- **Cause of Change:** All service changes shall have their cause or reason known and recorded as part of the change record, and a detailed description of the desired outcomes;
- **Source of Change:** The source of each change request shall be recorded in the change record;
- **Improvement Queue:** Problems are moved from the problem queue to the improvement queue following the development of solution statement, and in anticipation of a review of the proposed solutions and selection of the best set. Problems stay on the improvement queue until the recommended improvement has been successful implemented. Thus typically involves a change management procedure and a review of the change to verify the extent to which the desired results were achieved. Some changes may be sourced from the improvement queue;
- **Stewardship not Sponsorship:** Each change must have a sponsor in the form of an individual external to the change management group. Although it helps by ensuring the relevant information is collected and presented in a compelling manner, service change management does not justify a change, or obtain stakeholder or sponsorship support. Its primary duty is to steward and coordinate changes;
- **Scope of Change:** All change requests must include a statement of scope as to their known or likely effect;
- **Model Change:** Where possible, a model or template change request should be used to prepare a change request. Where one is not available, the change management group should consider whether the change being prepared may warrant the further and separate development of a model because it is likely to reoccur, and future efforts could be expedited as a result;
- **Change Proposal Statement:** Where the resources required to implement the change are extensive, especially with respect to change management group resources, a proposal statement is required to authorize further action by change management. This proposal statement will likely require fiscal approval, or the authority of executive management. The threshold for when a proposal statement is scenario specific and documented in each scenario;

- **Change Plan:** All change requests shall have a change plan, listing the step-by-step tasks to be completed for a successful change, the parties involved, the actions performed, how will the plan be monitored, and the communications plan. Change plans should specifically detail the approach to build the change work orders, and testing, the criteria and method for notifying interested parties of progress, and procedures to ensure efficient and successful routing of the work effort;
- **Backout Plan:** A change plan shall include a backout plan. A back-out strategy is mandatory for all change plans and needs to be explicit;
- **Communications Plan:** The change plan will include a communications plan, describing how all those affected by the change are consulted, what emotional factors need to be incorporated into the change plan about the impact, and how their involvement and support is fostered;
- **Escalation:** A change and any of its elemental work orders may be escalated to ensure progressive levels of responsibility and skill sets are involved in forming and delivering an appropriate response. It is the responsibility of the assigned Change Coordinator to ensure all escalations and notifications of events are completed in a timely manner, and in accordance with any plans;
- **Service:** The change should be related to a service or group of services;
- **Impact and Urgency:** The impact and urgency of a situation should be based upon the consumer scenario, and especially the activity, outcome, and politics of the community affected. If taken from a problem solution plan, its priority takes precedent and shall always form part of the change record;
- **Stakeholder Interest:** An impact statement should be created for each stakeholder affected by a problem situation;
- **Risk Assessment:** All change requests are subject to a formal assessment of the risk involved, including technical and practical feasibility. By default, the change management group assumes no risk. The risk starts and stays with the sponsor.
- **No Fault:** In extreme circumstances where a change request has to be expeditiously processed, perhaps as part of an emergency response or crisis management, the sponsor must sign "I hereby assume all risk" documentation;

- **Responsibility:** Although elements of a change may be assigned for work to various organizations it remains the sole responsibility of the change coordinator;
- **Correlation:** It is the responsibility of the Change Coordinator to relate any new change to existing change and form an aggregated view of the situation and overall impact;
- **Approval:** The approval of change is a multi-stage process, sometimes starting at the end of the problem management procedure. All changes are subject to a final approval stage, and the management level of the approvers is proportional to the amount of risk and cost involved in implementing the change;
- **Solution Plan:** Where the change is a implementing a solution plan provided by problem management, the work orders should be created using the information in the action plan, and the resources allocated according to the resource plan;
- **Test:** All testing of a change shall be performed according to criteria provided by a quality assurance responsibility, external to change management;
- **Situation and Continuity Plans:** All change plans must take into consideration existing situation management and continuity management planning;
- **Review:** All changes are subject to a post implementation review (PIR) and the creation of a PIR report.
- **Complete:** No change may be considered complete until all reports and documentation are finished;
- **Closure:** Change records may only be closed by the Change Manager;
- **Security Incident:** The procedures used to manage security related changes should be based upon the requirements and protocols of the security management responsibility;
- **Transfer of Command - Escalation:** The command function must be clearly established from the beginning of a change, as should the conditions under which command may be transferred. When command is transferred, the process must include a briefing that captures all essential information for continuing safe and effective operations. This information should be defined in the change plan;

- **Unified Command:** In changes involving multiple jurisdictions, a single jurisdiction with multiagency involvement, or multiple jurisdictions with multiagency involvement, Unified Command allows entities with different legal, geographic, and functional authorities and responsibilities to work together effectively without affecting individual agency authority, responsibility, or accountability. The unified command structure should be defined in the change plan and as part of a documented 'federated change management' policy.

Standardization:

- **Plain Language:** The description of the situation should use plain language, and terms most common to the consumer, user and affected parties. Although plain language may be appropriate during most changes, tactical language is occasionally warranted due to the nature of the change (e.g., during the application of a specific software 'patch'). The protocols for when tactical language may be used, including the use of special using specialized encryption, should be carefully described in the change plan.
- **Codes and Acronyms:** Shorthand descriptive codes should not be used for communication unless there is an agreed lexicon of code meanings in common use, instead all communications should be confined to essential messages. It is the responsibility of service change management to ensure information dissemination is timely, clear, acknowledged, and understood by all intended recipients;
- **Codes and Acronyms:** The use of acronyms should be avoided during changes requiring the participation of multiple independent third-parties or organizations;
- **Security:** When necessary, information may need to be encrypted so that security can be maintained;
- **Lexicon - Common Terminology:** All change documentation will use common terminology as defined within the Service Management Lexicon, designed to help define organizational functions, change facilities, resource descriptions, and position titles.

Facilities and Resources:

- **Locations and Facilities:** Service change management will be provided out of dedicated locations and secure facilities, offering confidentially of all information gathered during change management activities;
- **Resource Management:** Resources are defined as personnel, teams, equipment, supplies, and facilities available or potentially available for assignment or allocation in support of change management activities. The management of all changes will be subject to resource management disciplines, including throughout the lifecycle of a change, and reimbursement for resource use, as appropriate.
- **Dispatch/Assignment/Deployment:** Resources should only be allocated and staff should only instructed by an appropriate authority;
- **Resource Tracking:** Supervisors must record and report resource status changes as they occur.

Scope of Operation

The scope for the application and use of these procedures is defined as the management of a change as it relates to a service commitment, guarantee, or the ability to perform a customer activity. The scope of operation spans the entire lifecycle of a service change, from initiation to closure and reporting, and includes any continuity worthy event.

A change can include any addition, modification, replacement, or removal of an item recognized as being a component within a service infrastructure, and required to provide service.

To a large extent, the scope of operation is also determined by the context provided within a ***scenario action plan***. The scenario action plan, documented separately, provides specific instruction on how to apply these procedures to a scenario. Embedded within the scenario are:

- The cause or reason for the change;
- The consumer scenario, as appropriate;
- The related Solution Plan from problem management;
- The governance, including policies and decision-making criteria;
- Key performance measures, service level objectives, and change completion targets;
- Stakeholders and their individual interest.

Sometimes, as in the case of compliance with an international or national standard, or a regulation, a special procedure is mandated. When this happens, it will be necessary to create a change record and relate it to any other record required to help coordinate actions and communicate status and progress.

Unknown, or undocumented scenarios are excluded, and if action is taken, processed on a 'best effort', and no warranty basis. This means the standard operating procedures of service change management do not necessarily apply, and are likely replaced by a specialized routine, developed in real-time.

In every case, where a new scenario occurs, the change response will form the basis for a new scenario description.

The Relationship Continuous Improvement and Change Management

The concept of '*continuous improvement*' is at the center of many customer centric strategies designed to improve the quality and lower the cost of producing and supporting products and services.

A continuous improvement program (CIP) is often started by the detection and reporting of a problem in a process associated with building or delivering a product or service, or the identification of a defect in operations, or the quality or function of a product or service. Change management is the engine of continuous improvement, providing a ready means of implementation progressive changes as part of a formal improvement program.

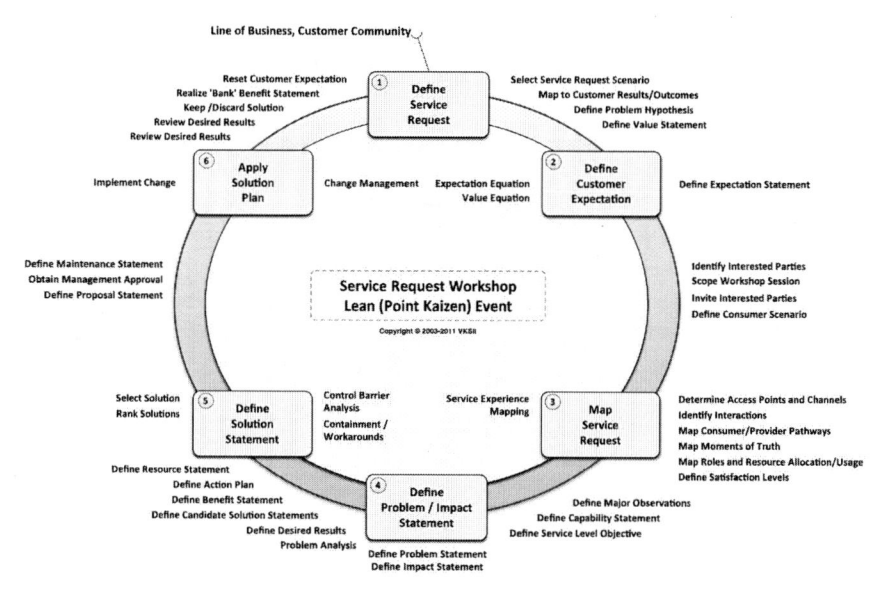

Figure 5: Continuous Improvement Cycle

In the above diagram, change management plays an integral role, forming step 6 of the overall continuous improvement cycle. Problem management spans steps 4 and 5, and is likely involved in the mapping, and inspection of the overall situation, commonly contained within a 'service request'.

Effective change management is the authorization mechanism for a continuous improvement program, and its span includes six-sigma, lean thinking, and other philosophies beneficial to service management strategies. Change management is the service management transformation and continuous improvement engine.

The Relationship Between Incident, Problem and Change

In some cases, there are three lifecycles active simultaneously: incident, problem and change. Once engaged, they each follow critical, resource and risk intensive paths. It is the responsibility of service incident management to ensure the interests of stakeholders affected by an incident situation are represented.

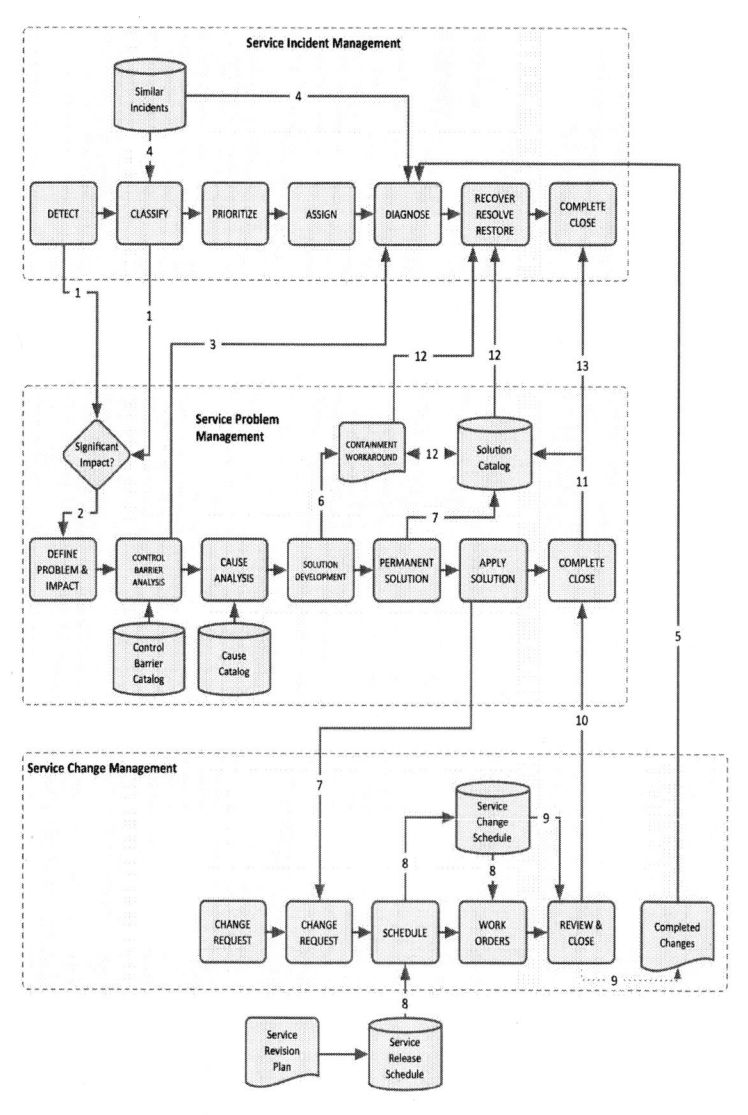

Figure 6: The Incident, Problem, and Change Lifecycle

It is the also responsibility of problem management to record as factually and completely as possible, the true impact of problematic events, and avoid any unnecessary distraction or diversion of problem and change management actions.

A general description of how changes progress through the lifecycles is as follows:

1. One or more incidents may cause, or suggest sufficient impact as to be noticed by problem management;
2. If it is determined an incident has significant enough impact, it causes an associated problem record to be created, and a problem and its impact defined;
3. Should the impact be significant enough to warrant invocation of cause analysis activities, the first assessment will be a 'control barrier analysis' effort. This activity involves special methods and may be performed as part of an initial diagnosis conducted within the incident management response;
4. Additional input to the initial diagnosis may include the matching of information and responses from similar incidents, which in turn may affect how the incident is classified;
5. During solution development, or as solution development activities and skills are invoked in response to incidents with significant impact, containment and workaround procedures and protocols may be created and made available as temporary resolutions. These are also added to the solution catalog. Only procedures contained within the solution catalog are authorized for use within the incident lifecycle;
6. When a permanent solution is developed it too is added to the solution catalog, providing visibility of its progress through to implementation to the incident lifecycle;
7. Permanent solutions are applied through a change request submitted to the change management system, and subject to the change lifecycle;
8. Once scheduled, and taking into consideration the prevailing service revision plan and service release schedule, the change is added to the service change schedule. The service change schedule is visible from within both the problem and incident lifecycles. Work orders are distributed and the change implemented;
9. Upon successful completion, post implementation review, and closure of the change request, information is created documenting changes completed. This is available to the incident lifecycle and may prove useful during the initial diagnosis activity;

10. When a change is completed, and again when closed after a successful review, its associated problem record is similarly completed and closed;
11. Following a successful review of the results within the problem lifecycle of a change, the solution catalog is updated and the information made available to the 3R stage of the incident lifecycle.
12. There is a correlation here between work orders completed in the change lifecycle and some or all activities performed during 3R, with 3R activities being authorized by a solution catalog entry;
13. Following a successful review of the results within the problem lifecycle of a change, the corresponding incident records may be completed and closed.

The Relationship Between Change and a Project

A change, or group of related changes may represent tasks defined within a project. If they do, then the work orders are built using information sourced from the project plan, and under the sponsorship and jurisdiction of the assigned project manager.

Target dates for completion, and the majority of the change plan, are developed using information in the project plan and tasks assignments. This includes dependencies, resource allocation and leveling, escalation and notification rules, and communication points.

How and when changes and the work orders they contain are completed, although defined within the change plan, will be entirely under the management control of the project manager. The project manager is also responsible for major aspects of risk assessment.

That said, a change coordinator will be assigned, and all other aspects of how the change is approved, scheduled and implemented, is governed by change management policies and procedures.

The Relationship between Change and Release

Release Management is the practice responsible for the planning, design, and operations management of releases. A release is one or more related changes to configuration items and components of a service infrastructure, created, tested, and deployed into a live environment all at the same time

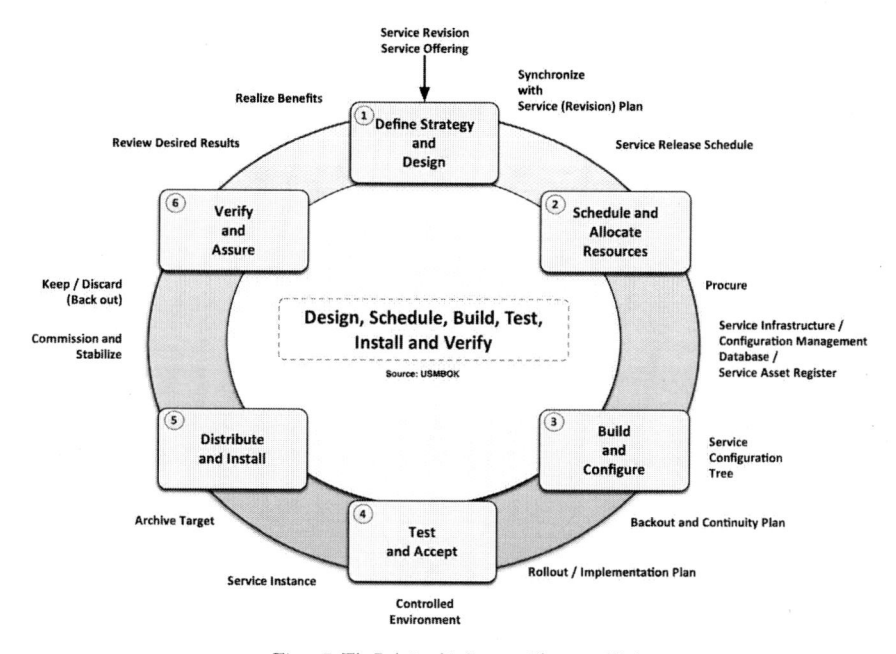

Figure 7: The Relationship Between Change and Release

In the above diagram, taken from service release management described in the USMBOK, the six major steps in the release lifecycle map closely to the major activities of change management. This is no coincidence.

All change, even a single change, should form part of a release, distributed, installed and verified as working by release management resources. Release management, when operational, is the workhorse of change management. Under change management governance and control, release management resources apply the change to a production, or 'live' service environment. No other person is allowed access.

Release management builds all work orders involved in staging infrastructure to production status, including the archiving of the target, or current versions of the components.

Typically under change management mandate and control, and as part of a release schedule carefully choreographed with service planners, release management resources archive the previous configuration, and the pull development class components into staging areas in preparation for pulling them into a controlled test environment (CTE). The CTE is where quality assurance is performed.

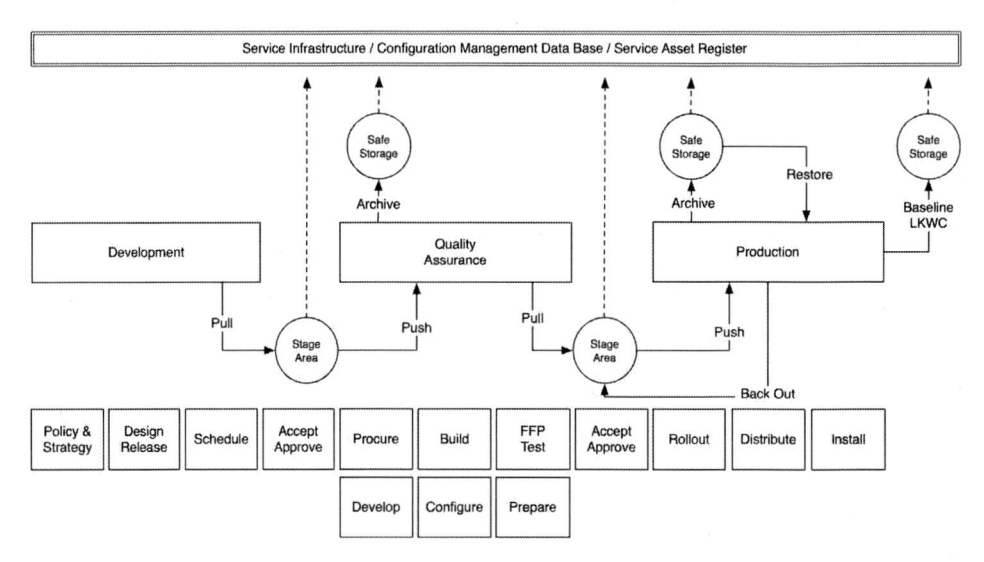

Figure 8: The Release Management 'PUSH', 'PULL' Methods

Once tested satisfactorily the tested components pulled from the CTE into staging areas in related release units (a release unit being a deliberately configured amount of change). At the scheduled time, the target production components are archived in such a way they can be used to restore the last known working configuration (LKWC), and the staged CTE releases pushed into production.

Rudimentary 'fit for purpose (FFP)' testing is performed in production to ensure all is working fine. If there are any problems, the backout and continuity plans may be invoked to restore the LKWC from the archive. All work is authorized and completed under a change management work order.

The Relationship between Change and Configuration

The current, past and planned location and status of all infrastructure components required to deliver and support a service, (also known as a configuration items), is maintained in a configuration management database (CMDB), managed by the service configuration management function.

The only way to add, move, change, or delete information in the CMDB is with the authorization of a change request work order.

A key concept, the 'zone of risk (ZOR)', integrates change and configuration management decision-making. The ZOR represents the complexity of the relationships of the configuration items within the CMDB, and their importance in supporting vital mission activities, and the level of risk encountered when changed.

The change procedures required to effect a change to the CMDB are proportional to the ZOR. This concept is described in more detail later in this document in the 'key concepts' section.

During audits of the CMDB to ensure its integrity and accuracy, the configuration management function will check the change record history to confirm an authorized change record exists for any differences since the last inspection, or baseline.

The change, configuration and release management practices work co-operatively, and under the governance of change management, to synchronize and record the movement, installation, and archiving of service components.

This page is left intentionally blank.

Roles and Responsibilities

Introduction

The personnel involved in performing service provider organization and support related actions are likely to change as the organizational structure and staffing undergoes its natural development. A *'Service Support Role Taxonomy'* should be used to cross reference the industry best practice role described within this publication, and the person or role currently performed within a support organization. In describing each role the procedures should support three perspectives:

- **Accountability or governance hierarchy**, representing the level of decision making responsibility within the organizational management structure;
- **Knowledge or functional capability**, representing the type and extent of skills, knowledge and abilities possessed by an individual, or required to perform an action;
- **Customer centricity**, describing the type of action performed and degree to which it is visible to the customer.

All actions are classified according to their level of visibility to customers. There are two classifications for provider side actions:

- **Front-Stage**, representing actions that are visible to the customer. These actions may be performed automatically as part of self-service capabilities, but typically involve direct customer contact and interaction by a support staffer. Front-stage actions are 'staged' and designed into an experience, and are candidates for 'moments of truth';
- **Back-Stage**, representing actions invisible to the customer, often supporting front-stage actions. Customer interactions should not directly drive back-stage actions.

Support processes are functional capabilities or communities of practice required to perform back-stage actions. Examples could include: Incident Management, Problem Management, Asset Management, or Procurement.

Roles, Persons and Organizations

In Daryl Conner's book "Managing at the Speed of Change"; he describes four distinct roles, representing an individual or group critical to the change process:

- **Sponsors:** they have the authority to sanction or legitimize change. They decide a change needs to happen. They provide proper reinforcement to ensure success and are responsible for creating an environment that enables timely, affordable change;
- **Agents:** responsible for actually making the change happen;
- **Targets:** these are impacted by the change and typically have to change in some way themselves. They must be educated and informed on the reason for change and involved appropriately;
- **Advocates:** they want the change but lack authority to sanction and support the change.

Specific to the procedures documented here, there are a number of principal roles and responsibilities defined within industry best practices for managing service related changes, they include:

- Sponsor: Change Sponsor (also known as the requester)
- Executive Level: Change Manager;
- Managerial Level: Change Coordinator;
- Operations Level: Change Agent;
- Support Process: Support Specialist.

The actions performed by each role are scenario specific.

Change Sponsor

A change sponsor is anyone who requires or prompts a change. This includes an entity that causes a problem, solved by a change request. Even if they do not directly request the solution, or even support the problem, as the cause they inherit the sponsor status. The responsibilities include:

- Authorizes the submission of a change request;
- Initiates, requests the change;
- Definition of the initial consumer scenario statement;
- Definition of the desired outcomes and success criteria for the change;
- Direct responsibility for disseminating key notifications of change progress to their own constituents;
- To ensure the change request, and as required risk assessment, is properly completed;
- To attend meetings and respond to communications as requested, and in a timely manner, to answer questions regarding a sponsored change request;
- To work cooperatively with the change management roles to support successful changes;
- Where sponsorship involves multiple parties, to work with partner sponsors to distribute and assign the work effort to help prepare, plan, coordinate and verify the successful completion of a change. Also, to distribute the risk stated, and funding required;
- To represent the needs of the community and seek approval for the change;
- To assist in verifying a successful change as part of the post implementation review activity;
- To provide funding for the change activities;
- To accept the risks associated with implementation, or to provide a statement confirming allocation and acceptance of risks to other parties;
- To accept responsibility for any negative impact resulting from a bad or failed change caused by inaccurate or incomplete sponsorship information.

It is important to note, although a change sponsor may commonly be an existing employee of the service provider organization or the enterprise organization, they may also be a third-party, such as contractor, supplier, or vendor.

Change Manager

The Change Manager provides executive level jurisdiction and governance over all service changes and the operation of a Change Management Group. The responsibilities include:

- The authorization of all changes;
- Sponsorship of all changes related to modifications to change management group policies and practices. They are not allowed to sponsor any other change;
- Acceptance of all risk on behalf of the change management group;
- Setting and management of performance targets, and definition of motivational schemes for the change management group;
- The operational management of the change management group and change coordinators;
- Soliciting the development of change plans;
- Monitoring of the service revision and release plans and resolution of conflicts with the published change schedule;
- The review and approval of change plans;
- Approval of modifications to change plans;
- Approval to escalate to the use of major incident, emergency response, and/or continuity plans;
- Liaison with customer management and executive levels;
- Liaison with third-party management and executive levels;
- Setting of priorities, and determination of competing change objectives;
- Conducting post implementation reviews to determine success of change, achievement of desired results, and effectiveness and efficiency of the change process;
- Authorization of non-standard communications such as information releases to the unauthorized third-parties, or the media;
- Ensuring all regulatory compliance and health and safety criteria are respected and included in change plans;
- Convening and chairing of change review board, and change review board high risk meetings;
- Denial of unacceptable or malformed change requests;

- Arbitration of change request priorities, resource conflicts, risk assessment differences, change constellation conflicts, and scheduling issues;
- Creation, approval and publication of the change schedule;
- Analysis of change records and reports to determine trends, possible problems;
- Authorization to invoke special change management procedures during major incidents, situation levels, backout of failed or bad changes, and active continuity plans;
- Closing of all change records;
- Promotion of the value of using change management practices to all candidate parties and key stakeholders, including all other service management areas of practice;
- Review of management reports and continuous improvement of policies, practices and protocols.

In addition, the Change Manager oversees the management of outbound communications relevant to change management activities, and cross-functional allocation and use of resources and assets.

For the Change Manager role to succeed it should have clear authority to manage changes across the service provider and partner organizations.

Change Coordinator

A Change Coordinator is a service support staffer assigned the responsibility of managing an individual change, or group of related changes, through their entire lifecycle. The Change Coordinator may be responsible for a number of changes at any one time, as part of a change portfolio, and specialize in a specific area of stakeholder operations. The Change Coordinator responsibilities include:

- End to end ownership of the change, from initiation following sponsorship, to completion. They are not allowed to be a change sponsor;
- Acting as the primary liaison during the change lifecycle with the Change Manager, the assigned change agents, and as necessary, the major incident manager, stakeholders, continuity coordinator, support specialists, and third-party resource;
- Where conditions are outside the boundaries of defined problem plan protocols, invocation of escalation and routines as required ensuring a proper response to the problem. This should include recognition and respect for any prevailing situation management and/or continuity management procedures and plans;
- Ensuring at all times the Change Manager has current information on a change and its progress and its progress, or lack thereof;
- Monitoring the change execution notifying the Change Manager of progress, any issues, and of the outcome of implementation of the change;
- Coordinating the movement of change requests through the various stages of the change lifecycle;
- Controlling and maintaining the change record and change management database to ensure its accuracy and currency;
- Review of the current improvement queue and synchronization with the change queue;
- The receipt, recording and initiation of an change request;
- Optional initiation of a change request on behalf of a sponsor;
- Ensuring a change is properly defined, with its impact clearly described, and sufficient information available to a successful assessment, review and implementation;
- Defining the scope of a change and filters out any changes that are out of scope, impractical, resource inefficient, or improperly formatted;

- Development and maintenance of the change plan to accompany each change request, to control the progress of the change through its lifecycle;
- Coordinating the development of a backout and/or continuity strategy as part of the change plan;
- Confirmation of the parties and stakeholders affected by the change, and inclusion in the change management lifecycle;
- Informing stakeholders and interested third-parties of the progress of the change;
- Creates a Post-Change Test Plan that can be executed to ensure the success of the change;
- The classification of each assigned change request;
- The prioritization of each assigned change request, where required based upon the predetermined prioritization of a problem record, or service request;
- Ensuring that the technical feasibility, risk and effect of the change have been adequately assessed;
- The commissioning of a risk assessment of the change from stakeholder impact, technical feasibility, and organizational change perspective;
- The assessment of the benefit of the change in relation to the cost;
- Estimation of the 'cost of change' and documentation of the revised benefit statement;
- The categorization of each assigned change based upon the predetermined category levels, and matching of change approval and review governance;
- Preparation, scheduling and submission of the change request to the appropriate approval board, and notification of the membership of its inclusion;
- Distribution of invitations to mandatory board review members to ensure proper review of the change, including the rationale for their involvement;
- Presentation of the change request to review board members in advance of meetings to allow prior consideration, responding to any questions;
- Documentation in the change record of all review board comments, questions, concerns, and decisions;
- Assignment and allocation of resource work effort and any additional resources of any kind required to progress the change once approved;

- Real-time arbitration of conflicting work effort assignments, allocations, and utilization;
- Communicating with the service support organization to inform them of any changed procedures, impending changes, and likely operational issues;
- Negotiating and scheduling the change request, synchronization with release and other schedules, notifying interested parties, including service support, of published schedule;
- Association of the change request with a specific release unit;
- Coordinating the building and distribution of all work orders;
- The solicitation of the development of situation management and service continuity plans;
- Coordinating the 'fit for purpose (FFP)' and acceptance testing of the change and verifying its correct operation prior to implementation;
- Coordination of each cross-functional implementation action and work effort and to ensure a common focus based upon the change plan criteria;
- Requiring a backout of a failed or bad change and optional invocation of a continuity plan;
- Coordination of work effort, escalation and governance across multiple jurisdictions;
- Monitoring the performance and efficacy of the change related work effort and supporting procedures;
- Identification of any issues in a problem response, the recording of an incident describing the issue, or the definition of a related problem statement;
- Where appropriate, initiating a review if criteria set is not met throughout the implementation of the change;
- Conducting post implementation reviews to determine the success of a change;
- Verifying and setting a change request status to complete, indicating the successful completion of all related work effort;
- Analyzes change records to determine any trends or apparent potential problems and seeks rectification with the relevant parties.
- Producing management information and reports regarding the change work effort that may be used to verify the actions taken to implement a change, satisfy audit or customer reporting requirements, and supporting continuous improvement;

- Suggesting and preparing submissions to the continuous improvement program for any opportunities to improve.

Generally, the Change Coordinator oversees the management of internal communications, and cross-functional allocation and use of resources and assets for implementing changes.

Change Agent

A Change Agent is any staff resource allocated and used to perform work authorized by a change plan. A change agent typically responds to a change related work order that has been approved and assigned by the change coordinator. The change agent works under the direct supervision of the change coordinator. A change agent's responsibilities include:

- Performing any action related to progression of change through its lifecycle, expect for the specific responsibilities assigned to the change manager and change coordinator roles, and including change risk assessment, building, testing, implementing, and reporting;
- Routing of work effort requests (work orders) to any other change agent, or change agent group queue;
- Assisting in the monitoring of the progress of change by updating the change history and change record as required;
- Assisting in ensuring current information is maintained and disseminated regarding the progress of a change;
- Ensuring appropriate levels of confidentiality are maintained;
- Assist in creation of the change plan;
- Ensuring all change agents are aware and adhere to the criteria and work effort described within a change plan;
- Risk assessment of a change;
- Attending the change review board meetings as required;
- Building of change work orders and verification that building of the change has been completed;
- Testing and quality assuring the change, verification that testing of the change has been completed, and documentation of any issues;
- Staging or distributing any element of the change;
- Installing or implementing any element of the change;

- Conducting any 'fit for purpose' or acceptance testing on behalf of the affected stakeholder;
- Updating the change log and change history to ensure accurate and timely information is available to the change coordinator and other change agents;
- Completing a backout of the change, if necessary;
- Recording and filing of all documentation, test results and reports associated with the change in a format suitable for, and accessible to, inspection and audit requirements.

Support Specialist

The support specialist role represents a person with special skills and knowledge of the service infrastructure and/or infrastructure management practices and processes. Support specialists possess knowledge, skills and abilities (KSA) that may be used anywhere within an authorized change.

Support specialists are mobilized and attached to temporary responder groups as part of the change plan, and are not under the direct supervision of the change coordinator, are involved in supporting back-stage actions, and normally responsible for:

- Technical support for infrastructure domains that include: software applications and systems, servers, storage, print, database, directory services, operations, hardware, software, network, facilities, and security;
- Planning the enterprise infrastructure architecture;
- Managing the service infrastructure, including real-time monitoring and proactive problem detection and mitigation;
- Development of diagnostic routines, containment and workaround procedures, and permanent solutions to problematic events
- Documenting and reporting infrastructure usage;
- Providing a meaningful response to an incident event to ensure a timely resolution.

Generally, support specialists do not perform front-stage actions, or interact directly with customer, or customer representatives.

Contractors and Vendors

A special note: contractors and vendors are required to adhere to the change control management policies and procedures. The following statement or its equivalent should appear in every contract:

"If the contractor/vendor requires modification to any part of the service infrastructure, for whatever reason, then they shall notify the change management group and request the approval to the proposed modification, such an agreement not to be unreasonably withheld. If such agreement is given, then the modification shall be carried out at a mutually convenient time using the established change management procedures".

Additional Organization Entities

There are also a number of organizational components or grouping of skills that may be convened to plan and coordinate the change:

- Change Management Group;
- Change Review Board;
- Change Review Board for High Risks.

It is important to note that one individual may perform several roles, and alternatively several people could fulfill one role (for example, the task of assessing a change might be performed by several people). Roles therefore should not be confused with persons.

The Change Management Group

The Change Management Group (CMG) is the organizational unit responsible for the approval and administration of all service changes. They are responsible for all activities relating to Change Management administration including:

- Initiation, assessing, approving, and coordination of the implementation of all changes;
- Maintaining an accurate record of all changes;
- The elimination and avoidance of any unauthorized changes;
- The constant review of the opportunity queue;
- The administration of the change queue and change schedule;
- The coordination of all activities related to the implementation of a change;
- The continuous review an improvement of change management procedures.

The CMG establishes a formal sub-group – the 'change review board' to formally review change requests and ensure they are appropriately tracked and progressed.

The review board may also ensure suitable priorities are assigned, and resources allocated, and provide oversight into the post implementation review of changes. The review board also operates as the final arbiter of change requests.

Change Review Board (CRB)

The Change Review Board (CRB) is a forum for the review of all 'normal' change requests. The CRB is responsible for assessing the risk, impact, priority and resource requirements of proposed changes and advising the Change Manager as to whether the change should be approved.

The Change Review Board (CRB) is an advisor to the Change Manager. Only the change manager can approve a change request.

The Change Coordinators must regularly review and present to the CRB all outstanding changes awaiting approval. If necessary, the priority levels of these changes may be adjusted by the CRB to take into account any changes of circumstance, age of the request, and other issues such as the availability of resources and schedules.

Generally, the CRB can 'convene' virtually, using remote access technology to review the change requests scheduled for review, and whether meeting virtually or in person, should ensure satisfactory answers exist to the following common questions:

- What is the nature of the change?
- How does the change support the vision of the organization?
- How does the change better align our organization with its objectives?
- What are the risks of making the change, what can go wrong and what are the consequences, and to whom?
- How will the change impact our organization?
- Why is this change necessary?
- Why is this change happening now?
- What is wrong with what we are doing today?
- What will happen if we don't change?
- What's in it for us?
- What's in it for me?
- What's in it for our customer?

The CRB may convene after the implementation of a change as part of the post implementation review activity, and further help verify:

- The change has had the desired effect and met its objectives;
- Stakeholders are satisfied with the results;
- There have been no unexpected or undesirable side-effects;
- The resources used to implement the change were as planned and can now be released;
- The reasons or a bad or failed change are known and recorded.

The constituency of the CRB varies dependent on the change request scenario under review. Members of the CRB are invited to attend based upon the queue of change request scheduled for review.

The CRB reviews all 'emergency', or 'urgent' change requests, and helps the change manager set the criteria for invoking the change review board for high risk (CRB-HR).

Change Review Board for High Risk (CRB-HR)

The change review board for high risk (CRB-HR) has the same mandate as the CRB, expect for change request that have an exceptional or unacceptable level of risk, or require a substantial investment of change management and associated resources.

The CRB-HR is a special forum comprised of senior executive management, and the Change Manager. Additional members are invited to take part on an as required basis, and should at least include the change sponsor.

The CRB has jurisdiction over what change are sent to the CRB-HR. The Change Manager is the final arbiter, and cannot be forced to approve changes under any circumstances that are felt to be of high risk or have a similarly high cost.

Generally, the CRB can 'convene' virtually, using remote access technology to review the change requests scheduled for review, and whether meeting virtually or in person, should ensure satisfactory answers exist to the following common questions:

- Why are we reviewing this change?
- What is specifically exceptional about this change?
- What concerns do the CRB and change manager have regarding the change?
- How are these concerns satisfied or overcome?
- What information and assurances do we need from the sponsor, have they been provided?
- Do we recommend the continuance of the change and accept the risks and costs included in the change request?

The change may be complex, difficult to implement, have a known risk of significant impact should it fail, have incomplete or unsatisfactory supporting documentation, be sponsored by an organization with political muscle that may also prefer to circumvent mandated change procedures, or prefer to use their own.

As stated earlier, the Change Manager and the CRB can set the criteria, but typically the primary criteria for invoking the CRB-HR are high risk, caused for whatever reason.

The Continuity Response Team

A continuity response team is also a temporary organizational structure and governance framework designed to respond to a specified continuity plan procedure. When and how such a team is invoked and what actions they perform as a countermeasure, is the subject of separate continuity planning documentation.

This page left intentionally blank.

Lexicon

Introduction

The following key terms are used as part of the service change management practice:

- **Improvement Queue:** the list or prioritized queue of opportunity statements;
- **Service Change:** the process of moving the state of an element of the service infrastructure (also termed a configuration item or 'CI'), from its current state to a new desired state;
- **Change Plan:** Documentation of the step-by-step tasks to be completed for a successful change, the parties involved, the actions performed, how will the plan be monitored, and progress communicated. Change plans should specifically detail the approach to build the change work orders, and testing, the criteria and method for notifying interested parties of progress, and procedures to ensure efficient and successful routing of the work effort;
- **Change Proposal:** Authorizes further action by change management where the resources required to implement the change are extensive. This proposal statement will likely require fiscal approval, or the authority of executive management. The threshold for when a proposal statement is scenario specific and documented in each scenario;
- **Consumer Scenario:** A description of the context of performing an activity to achieve a successful customer outcome. Typically described in detail from a consumer perspective;
- **Vital Mission Activity (VMA):** An activity performed by a stakeholder with some tangible significance and effect on the achievement of an outcome. A VMA must be qualified as such through detailed documentation, describing the conditions surrounding its performance and its relationship to a key performance target, and/or objective;

- **Stakeholder Interest:** A stakeholder is a person, group, or organizations that must somehow be taken into consideration when making a decision, performing an activity, or conducting any form of analysis, reporting, or assessment. Stakeholder interest describes the relationship, and how they make be affected. An interest may be positive or negative, and could be defined materially (loss of property, opportunity for profit), cultural, or even emotional. The interest may be further classified as primary, secondary, typically linked to organizational objectives, or tertiary, related to personal objectives;
- **Impact:** A measure of the positive or negative effect upon a stakeholder and their ability to achieve a desired outcome or objective;
- **Urgency:** The necessary speed with which a situation, such as an incident, service request, change or problem, should be resolved;
- **Change Constellation:** A possible, or known network of related change requests;
- **Risk Assessment:** The activity of assessing the probability of something happening and having an impact or consequence upon one or more stated objectives;
- **Risk Priority Number (RPN):** The result of a risk assessment activity, representing the relevant importance of mitigate or eliminating a condition, or risk. A measure used within the Failure Mode Effect Analysis (FMEA) technique to help prioritize causes or weaknesses in a system design, with values ranging from 1 (absolute best) to 1000 (absolute worst). The RPN is the product of three FMEA ratings:
  - **Severity (S):** severity, occurrence and detection, a numerical subjective estimate of how severe the customer (next user) or end user will perceive the EFFECT of a failure
  - **Occurrence (O):** Sometimes termed LIKELIHOOD, is a numerical subjective estimate of the LIKELIHOOD that the cause, if it occurs, will produce the failure mode and its particular effect
  - **Detection (D):** Sometimes termed EFFECTIVENESS, a numerical subjective estimate of the effectiveness of the controls to prevent or detect the cause or failure mode before the failure reaches the customer. The assumption is that the cause has occurred.

- **Priority:** a value used to represent the relative importance of an item when compared with others. Commonly used to sequence a work effort within one or more organizational units;
- **Change Queue:** A list, or queue of changes, representing their status and progress within the change lifecycle, and inclusive of the stages INITIATED to COMPLETED (see major activities section later in this document);
- **Change Schedule:** A timetable of approved changes. The schedule should document changes that have recently occurred and are planned within specific periods of time. The schedule is the definitive agenda for when changes will happen and under the direct authority of the Change Manager. It can also be joined to the change queue to show the 'pipeline' of changes, from pre-approved through to completed;
- **Change Slot:** A period of time on a change schedule within which a change can happen and a specific amount of risk is accepted. The slots may be arranged by line of business, line of service, location, service, community or even vital mission activity;
- **Work Order:** A request for resources, typically initiated by a build and including a detailed description of the activities needed to complete a task within a change. For example, to assess the risk, or vote for the approval of a change request;
- **Test Plan:** Descriptions of the sequence of tests to be performed to determine the quality of a change build, and verify the readiness for change to be implemented. The test plan includes the actions to be performed and roles required for each action;
- **Backout Plan:** The actions to be performed should a change fail, or have unsatisfactory results;
- **Change History:** A chronological timeline of auditable information related to a change that records what was done, when, by whom and why;
- Release: one or more related changes to configuration items, identified as elements of a service infrastructure, which must be implemented together.

A more comprehensive explanation for each of the above terms may be found in the USMBOK's 'Service Management Lexicon'.

This page left intentionally blank.

Key Artifacts

Introduction

An artifact is tangible evidence of human activity and often associated with a deliverable created, owned and primarily used by a practice area. The key artifacts associated with service change management include:

- Service Change Record;
- Unique identification scheme for change records;
- Model Change;
- Standard Change;
- Change Queue;
- Change Catalog;
- Change Schedule;
- Work Order;
- SCARI Chart;
- Service change report catalog items.

This section provides additional information on each of these artifacts in turn.

The Service Change Record

The following information recorded each service change request includes:

- A unique reference number;
- Title – short title for reference
- Description – short description
- The origin;
- Initiation timestamp;
- The cause;
- The related improvement queue entry;
- The sponsor and contact information;
- Recording method and recording analyst or agent;
- Change status (for example: model, standard, active, pending, queued);
- The assigned change coordinator, contact information and status;
- The scope of the change;
- The related project;
- Change constellation membership;
- The related authorized change plan;
- The related change model;
- Timestamps for detection, stage entry and exits, status changes;
- The classification and sub-classifications;
    - The affected community;
    - The affected vital mission activity;
    - The related service infrastructure, or configuration item;
    - The related service;
- The stated urgency;
- The stated impact;
- The requested priority;
- The initial, default service level entitlement;
- The initial, default escalation ruleset;
- The initial, default notification method and messaging;
- The change category and sub-category;
- Approval method and board;
- Related work orders, and work order status, including risk assessments;
- The service contract;

- Related service level entitlement;
- Escalation ruleset;
- Notification ruleset and methods;
- The situation level;
- The related risk statement;
- The resource availability status;
- The calculated priority;
- The target time for completion;
- The related schedule slot reference;
- The scheduled time for completion;
- Contact information for affected parties;
- The build membership;
- The related test plan;
- The related release unit and package;
- The related backout and continuity plan;
- Related post implementation review plan;
- Related post implementation test plan;
- 2C timestamps, classifications for complete and close stages;
- Related completion interview;
- Related closure interview;
- Related satisfaction survey;
- Related assessment procedure.

The Unique Identification Scheme

Each element within the change management system requires unique identification; this includes the overarching change record. Each record should be uniquely identified, allowing for efficient and secure storage, retrieval and reference.

The scheme could be as simple as a numeric sequence. The level of sophistication of a scheme, and whether it can be enhanced to improve indexing and reporting, will likely be dependent on client software capabilities.

Model Change

A model change is a template for managing a change, consisting of proven and repeatable procedures for processing a specific type of change request.

A change model may consist of detailed information on the probable cause or reasons, work orders, estimated effort and turnaround time, risk and impact analysis requirements, pre-defined activities, governance, success criteria, and cost estimates.

Standard, Pre-Approved Change

A change consisting of proven and repeatable procedures for processing a specific type of change request, and one that does not require review at the time of submission by the CRB or CRB/HR.

Typically, the change has been previously determined to have little or no significant associated risk. Often a pre-approved change may be automatically applied as a scheduled event. The concept of pre-approving a change is used to remove and replenish spare infrastructure to accelerate a recovery, resolution or restoration activity.

A standard change consists of detailed information on the probable cause or reasons, *work orders*, estimated effort and turnaround time, risk and impact analysis requirements, pre-defined activities, governance, success criteria, and cost estimates.

A standard change is a candidate for automation and may be scheduled as a pre-approved change

Change Queue

The following information should be maintained regarding change queue entries:

- A unique identifier;
- Related change record;
- Timestamps for date added to queue and for any stage or state change for progression through queue;
- Last status;
- Current status;
- Next status;
- Sponsor and submitter contact information;
- Optional target date for exiting queue;
- Related improvement queue entry;
- The status of the procedure indicating its availability of use;
- Current management opinion (may be based upon a vote to authorize further action and progression);
- Management review/opinion team members;
- Feedback in the form of comments, opinions and Q&A from review team.

Change Catalog

The following information should be maintained regarding change models and standard requests recorded in the change catalog:

- A unique identifier;
- The name of the change model or standard;
- Time stamp related information indicating its creation date, last updated date, and current currency;
- Related change model records;
- Related standard change records;
- Related change management procedure for maintenance;
- Owner, assigned change coordinator, support contact, developer;
- The status of the record indicating its availability of use;
- Last use date, indication of degree of success;
- Related changes for which procedure was used;
- Authorized users and conditions or criteria for invocation, including specific scenarios if appropriate.

Change Schedule

This is a calendar of approved change request events for a specific forward-looking period, and also showing the most recently completed changes. It is maintained in real-time with look-ahead based upon planning cycle - 'horizons', and contains full details on planned/authorized changes. The information maintained regarding change schedule entries should include:

- A unique identifier;
- A change slot identifier;
- A change slot description;
- A change slot time period of operation;
- A change slot status;
- Related change queue record;
- Related change request;
- Timestamps for date added to schedule and for any stage or state change for progression through the lifecycle;
- Timestamps for last schedule update, next update.

It is feasible the change schedule describes the change slots available and scheduled changes for a specific location, area of business or enterprise operations, or any subset of the service portfolio, which are aggregated to provide a 'federated' view.

Work Order

A work order is an integral part of a change request and represents a request for resources to perform a change related activity or task. For example, to assess the risk of a change, or vote for its approval. The information recorded for a work order should include:

- A unique identifier;
- Title – short title for reference
- Description – short description;
- The related change record;
- Related work orders and their relationship, including dependencies;
- The type of work order;
- Information and instructions on how to complete the work order;
- An estimate of the effort to complete the work order;

- An assignment of skills or roles required to complete the work orders;
- An estimate of the resource cost;
- The status of the resource with respect to availability, for example 'ready for work', 'on vacation', 'Being purchased', or similar;
- Time stamp related information indicating its assignment or allocation date;
- Known supervisor contact information;
- A proportional indicator, describing the level of effort expected or available, as in project management leveling;
- Supporting commentary text;
- Signatories authorizing the request for and assignment of a resource.

SCARI Chart

A straightforward and useful tool presented as a table or grid, used for identifying the levels of responsibility of any role involved in an activity, procedure or process. The term SCARI is an abbreviation for 'supportive', 'consulted', 'accountable', 'responsible', and 'informed'.

The chart is with the activities or steps in a process on one axis and the roles on the other. One of the SCARI abbreviations is used at each intersection of activity and role to describe the level of responsibility that role has in each activity.

The Service Change Report Catalog Items

The Service Change Report catalog is a subset of the overall Report Catalog. Like the Report Catalog, this provides a formal specification of the reports authorized for publication and use, by each service.

- A unique identifier;
- Time stamp related information indicating its creation date, last updated date, and current currency;
- Related change request records associated with maintenance of the catalog;
- Related change management procedure for maintenance;
- Owner, assigned change coordinator, support contact, developer;
- Report title;
- Description of the report purpose, intended message;
- Report type, for example, internal or external;
- Scope of information, including geographic, location, service, key performance measures discussed, infrastructure, policy, procedure, vital mission activity, or artifact involved;
- Level of confidentiality;
- Publishing organization;
- Target audience, which individuals, communities, business unit, or organizations;
- Published format;
- Distribution method;
- Interval scope, period of time or duration contained within report information;
- Frequency of production and publishing cycle;
- Policies and procedures for creation and maintenance;
- Related change request records associated with maintenance of the report;
- Related reports;
- Related archive for previous versions.

Concepts and Methods

Introduction

This section introduces some of the key concepts and methods used by the service change management practice area, including:

- Change Equation;
- Change Lifecycle;
- Problem-Change Lifecycle;
- Zones of Risk;
- Change Slot;
- Cost of Change.

The Change Equation

The change equation illustrates the factors involved in determining the likelihood of gaining sufficient support to be approved and completed successfully. The following diagram, adapted from one Beckhard and Harris themselves derived from earlier sources, illustrates the key elements.

Likelihood of Change = [Level of Impact Dissatisfaction with Status Quo | Desirability, Benefit of Proposed Change and Future State | Possibility, Practicality, Timing of Change (Risk + Disruption)] > Emotional Investment, Cost of Changing

Derived from Beckhard and Harris Change Formula (1987)

Figure 9: The Change Equation

The likelihood of a change happening is dependent upon the level of impact, and dissatisfaction experienced by each stakeholder or observer, with the status quo, compared with the desirability or benefit associated with the future state the change proposes.

Add the possibility of change (perhaps due to political influences or complexity), the practicality (capability and available skill sets), and timing of a change, and the risk and possible disruption it entails.

All of this must be greater than the emotional investment, or cultural shock inherent in current mindsets and operations, and the cost of the change, to improve the likelihood. A simple equation on the outside, the benefit outweighs the cost, but subtle in including the often hidden emotional and organizational impact.

Change Lifecycle

The change lifecycle is the life history and descriptive account of the progression of a service change through successive stages of activity. The change lifecycle is used to track and communicate the status and progress of a change, from its original initiation to closure. The following diagram provides an overview of the interaction and interoperation between the change lifecycle, and its closest neighbors, the incident and problem lifecycles.

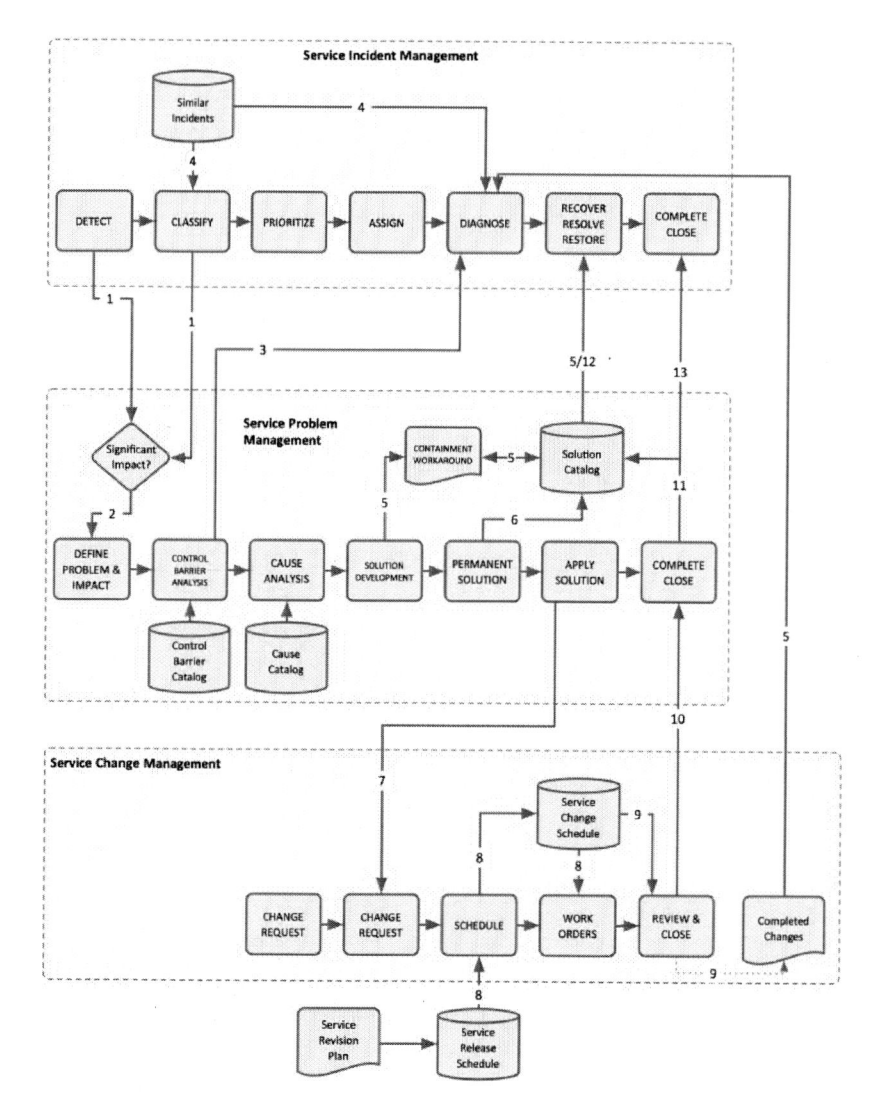

Figure 10: The Change Lifecycle

A general description of how the three lifecycles commonly interact is as follows:

1. One or more incidents may cause, or suggest sufficient impact as to be noticed by problem management;
2. If it is determined an incident has significant enough impact, it causes an associated problem record to be created, and a problem and its impact defined;
3. Should the impact be significant enough to warrant invocation of cause analysis activities, the first assessment will be a 'control barrier analysis' effort. This activity involves special methods and may be performed as part of an initial diagnosis conducted within the incident management response;
4. Additional input to the initial diagnosis may include the matching of information and responses from similar incidents, which in turn may affect how the incident is classified;
5. During solution development, or as solution development activities and skills are invoked in response to incidents with significant impact, containment and workaround procedures and protocols may be created and made available as temporary resolutions. These are also added to the solution catalog. Only procedures contained within the solution catalog are authorized for use within the incident lifecycle;
6. When a permanent solution is developed it too is added to the solution catalog, providing visibility of its progress through to implementation to the incident lifecycle;
7. Permanent solutions are applied through a change request submitted to the change management system, and subject to the change lifecycle;
8. Once scheduled, and taking into consideration the prevailing service revision plan and service release schedule, the change is added to the service change schedule. The service change schedule is visible from within both the problem and incident lifecycles. Work orders are distributed and the change implemented;
9. Upon successful completion, post implementation review, and closure of the change request, information is created documenting changes completed. This is available to the incident lifecycle and may prove useful during the initial diagnosis activity;

10. When a change is completed, and again when closed after a successful review, its associated problem record is similarly completed and closed;
11. Following a successful review of the results within the problem lifecycle of a change, the solution catalog is updated and the information made available to the 3R stage of the incident lifecycle.
12. There is a correlation here between work orders completed in the change lifecycle and some or all activities performed during 3R, with 3R activities being authorized by a solution catalog entry;
13. Following a successful review of the results within the problem lifecycle of a change, the corresponding incident records may be completed and closed.

The Problem-Change Cycle

There is a strong correlation and needed integration between the activities of the problem and change management practices. In the following diagram, the 'plan-do-change-act' cycle of learning created by Dr, Shewhart, and popularized by Edward Deming, is used to show how the two can combine to powerful effect.

In the following diagram, a customer event (0) – shown at the bottom lower right, can initiate a problem and opportunity to improve (1). Once the impact (2) is known and added to the problem/opportunity statement, the customer's special criteria (3) are included along with the service provider goal (4), such as complete within a time period or budget.

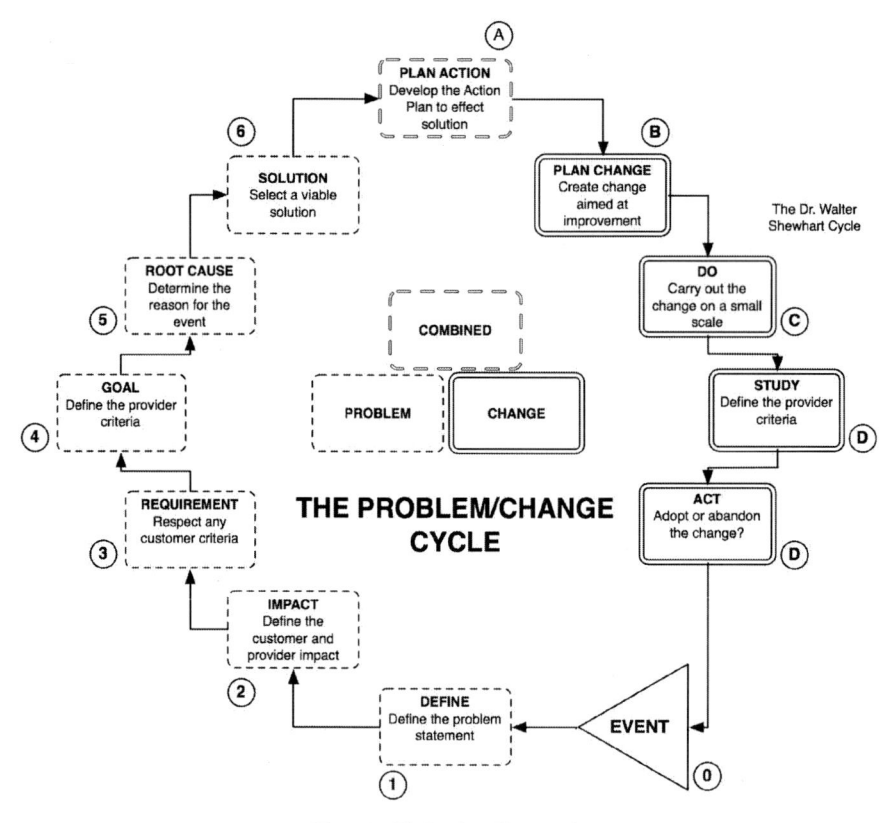

Figure 11: The Problem-Change Cycle

The causes of the problem are investigated and a root cause sought. A solution is developed and selected and an action plan created (A).

The solution and action plan are submitted to the change management procedures for implementation. Implementation is achieved by planning for the change (B), 'doing' the change (C), studying the results (check), and deciding whether it is kept, or discarded (D).

Zones of Risk

This concept relates to the intensity and rigor of the change procedure being practice aligned with degree of risk to service configuration service levels. The more risk, the greater the due diligence performed. A 'risk' assessment should include review of the configuration in the form of a component failure impact analysis (CFIA) or similar.

ZONES OF RISK

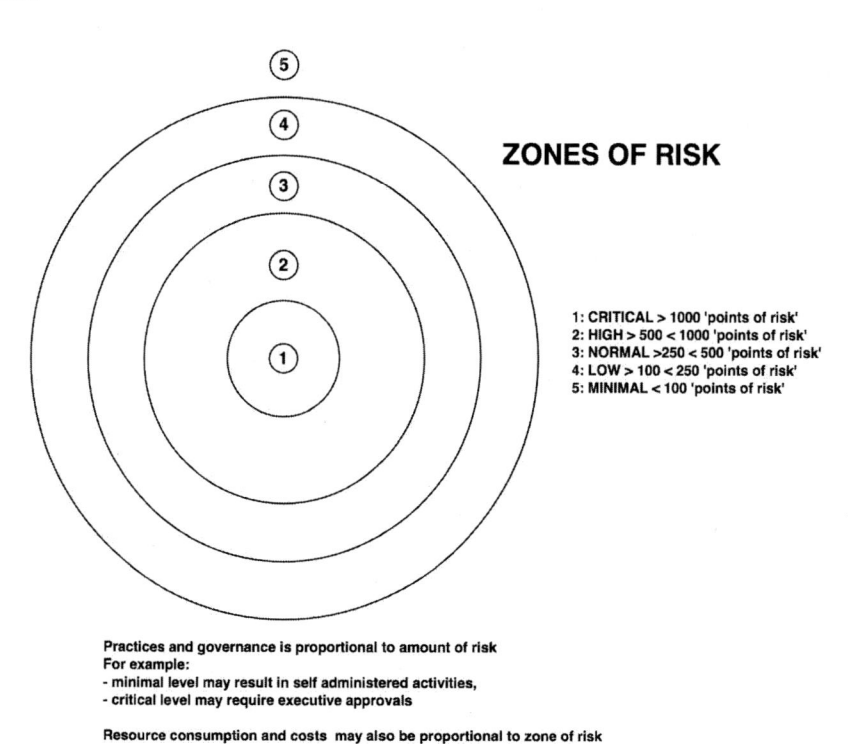

1: CRITICAL > 1000 'points of risk'
2: HIGH > 500 < 1000 'points of risk'
3: NORMAL >250 < 500 'points of risk'
4: LOW > 100 < 250 'points of risk'
5: MINIMAL < 100 'points of risk'

Practices and governance is proportional to amount of risk
For example:
- minimal level may result in self administered activities,
- critical level may require executive approvals

Resource consumption and costs may also be proportional to zone of risk

Figure 12: Zones of Risk

The previous 'zones of risk' diagram illustrates the concept of increasing zones of risk, mapped to an increasingly comprehensive change procedure.

The zones may be service or infrastructure specific and defined to correspond to how critical an item is to the provision of a service.

The change procedure should offer a level of protection relative to the degree of risk. Infrastructure domain managers should be responsible for sponsoring an item into the appropriate zone – not Change or Configuration Management.

The ZOR concept allows a proportionally higher amount of effort, and cost of change, to be applied to the riskier changes.

It also allows 'impacts' to work as a 'gravitational pull' to the proper zone. By this, it is meant that a change sponsor may have requested a lower risk zone and then suffer a failure and a consequential impact to service levels.

On the retry or subsequent attempt they may defer to a change procedure for a more intensive, risk-laden zone. The ZOR concept also means:

- Change practice and policies are proportional in bureaucracy to the amount of risk indicated by the zone in which a configuration item resides;
- A *minimal* level zone residency may imply self administered activities, and a *critical* level zone residency will require stringent procedures and executive level approvals;
- Zone residency will dictate whether continuity requirements should be revisited.

Change Slot

A 'change slot' is period of time defined to a change schedule within which a change can happen. Each change slot has a maximum amount of risk, based upon an arbitrary risk value system. A zero-risk slot would equate to a 'black-out' or no-change period.

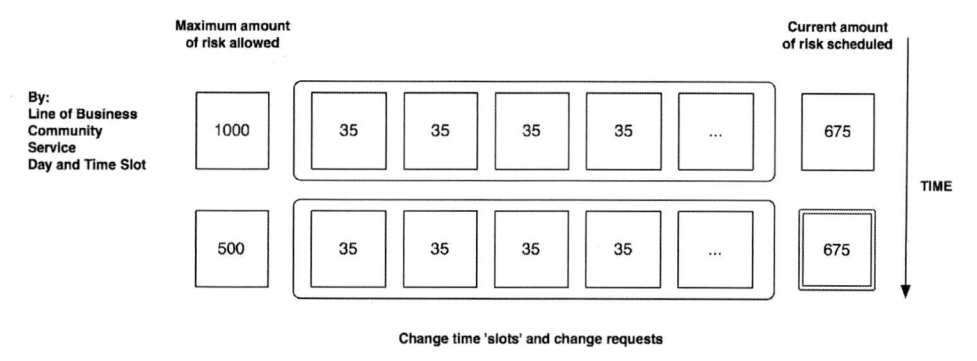

Figure 13: The Change Slot

The total value of all the changes scheduled for a slot can be totaled, and if greater than the allowable maximum, scheduled based upon priority, moving the lower priority changes to an alternate slot. The change schedule must be fully integrated with the service calendar, release and maintenance schedules.

The Cost of Change (CoC)

Changes represent one of the most common forms of expense and one of the largest hidden costs of any organization. Irrespective of the benefit derived as a result, all changes require resources to implement, they have an expense, and they incur 'cost'.

The total expense of all activities and resources consumed to affect a change request is termed the 'cost of change (CoC)' and is estimated, planned and calculated as part of managing the change.

The difference between the estimated and planned cost of change, and the actual cost, is a key performance measure, and indicator as to the effectiveness of the change management practices.

This page is left intentionally blank.

Inputs

Introduction

The sources of input to the service change management practice include:

- Problem records;
- Scenario action plan;
- Improvement queue records;
- Service requests;
- Service catalog;
- Service infrastructure catalog;
- Service contracts;
- Supplier contracts;
- Operations contracts;
- Other standard operating procedures;
- Master staff list;
- Resource plan;
- Action plan;
- Service revision plan;
- Service release schedule;
- Plans, policies and protocol documentation.

The inputs identified here are likely key outputs from other service management practice areas.

This page left intentionally blank.

Outputs

Introduction

Key outputs represent significant deliverables derived from the performance of the major activities of a practice on a day-to-day and longer-term basis. Outputs are typically in the form of what is termed an *artifact* or 'evidence of human activity'. Examples may include updated items (such as a change schedule or release unit) or information items (plans, policies, and procedures). The service change management practice generates a number of key outputs, including:

- Change record;
- Change proposal statement;
- Change plan;
- Risk assessment statement;
- Updated change queue;
- Change approval statement;
- Impact statement;
- Change schedule;
- Confirmed action plan;
- Work orders;
- Arbitration statements;
- Backout plan;
- Communications plan;
- Test plan;
- Release plan;
- Benefit statement;
- Various reports.

The outputs identified are likely key inputs to both this practice and one or more of the other service management practice areas. Information items such as reports are discussed in the 'performance management framework' section of this publication.

This page left intentionally blank.

Major Activities

Introduction

This section describes the major activities performed by this practice area and the preferred sequence of actions to be performed in response to a service change. A major activity is defined as a collection of related tasks or actions (activities) performed to achieve a stated outcome or set of objectives. The following diagram represents the major activities covered.

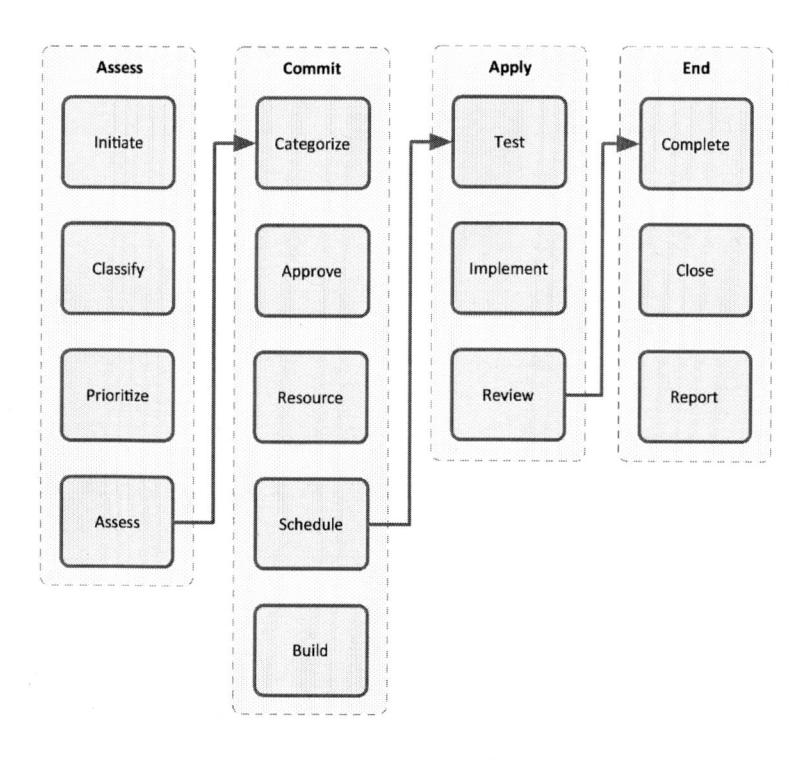

Figure 14: Major Activities

Although a sequence is suggested, it is more often the case an activity remains 'active' in that is can be continually performed during the entire lifecycle, up to and including the 'close' activity. An example of this is the 'initiate' activity, invoked by a sponsor to begin the process of recording information about a change request.

For each major activity, this section describes the activity, its objectives, major influences, sub-activities, inputs, outputs, and key roles and responsibilities. The major activities span four phases:

- Assess;
- Commit;
- Apply;
- and End phase.

Assess Phase

The 'assess' phase spans four major activities, from the initiation of the change request, through prioritization, to risk assessment.

Commit Phase

The 'commit' phase spans five major activities, from the categorization, through approval, to build.

Apply Phase

The 'Apply' phase spans three major activities, which together are responsible for testing, implementing and reviewing the relative success of the change request.

End Phase

The 'End' phase spans three major activities, which together signal the end of all activities related to the completion of all change related activities, verification of stakeholder satisfaction, and providing management feedback via reporting.

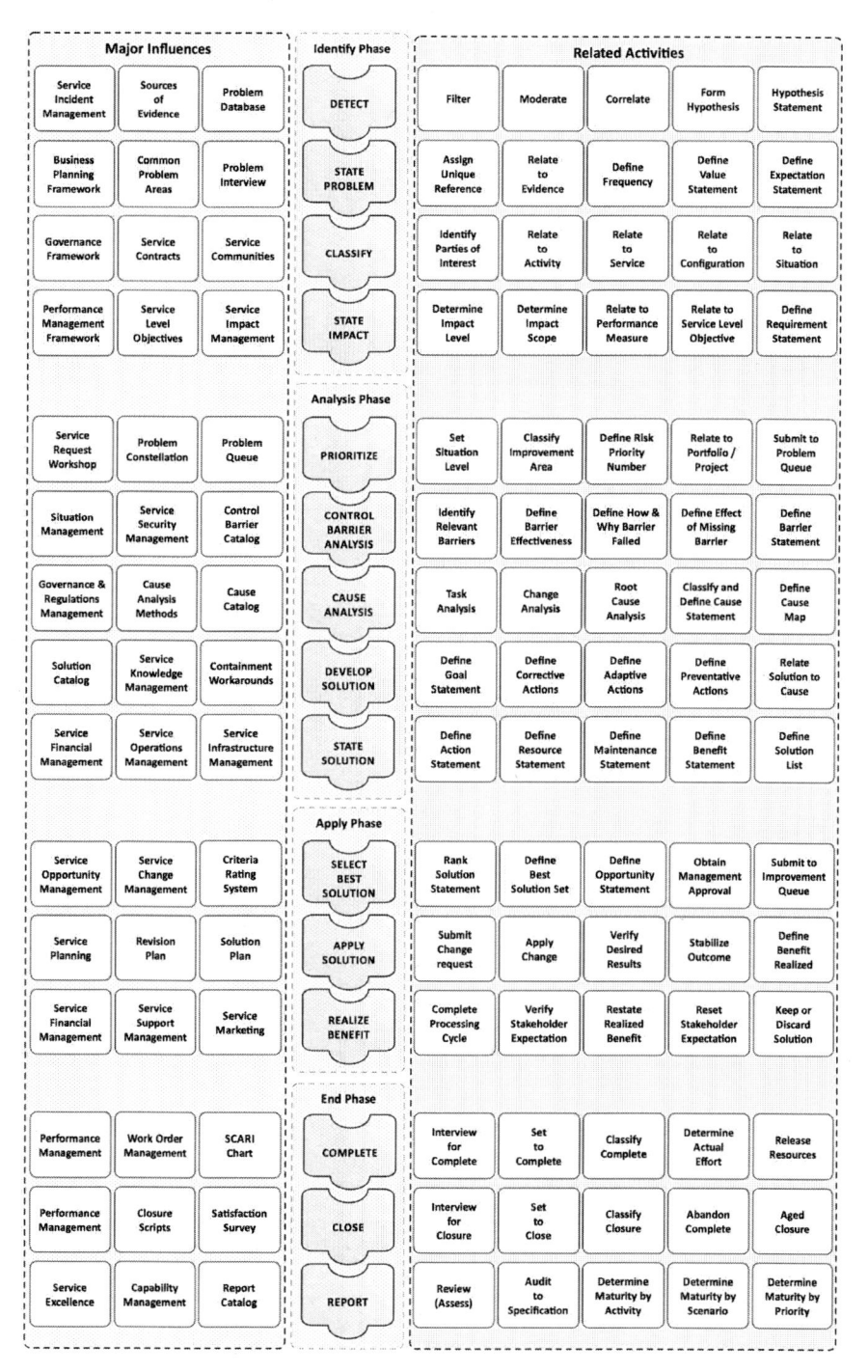

Figure 15: Major Activities - 'Yellow Stripe'

How to Interpret the Major Activity Information

In the descriptions of the major activities, the diagrams each contain a number of common elements, including:

- **Major influences:** A major influence represents other knowledge domains, knowledge areas within a domain, or specific artifacts that have a significant influence over the activity. The influence may be in the form of a key input, policy statements, or perhaps procedural integration or interoperation. In all cases these are three that are highlighted and favored, they do not represent a complete list;
- **Major activity:** A major activity performed by the practice. Up to fifteen major activities are described for each practice area. The objectives of each are described along with its key inputs and outputs, and actors;
- **Related Activities:** Five significant related activities, also termed sub-activities, are provided for each major activity, providing comprehensive guidance on the work effort involved in completing the major activity. Similar to the major influences, these represent the more common or significant, and not a complete list of sub-activities.

The general currency and completeness of each major influence can significantly affect the provider's capability to successfully perform the major and related activities. As such, they should be regularly assessed, and subjected to period inspection by neutral third-parties, perhaps as part of a formal audit, and they should also be assessed during normal operational use.

There is an implied 'stage entry' and 'stage exit' criteria for each major activity and sub-activity. This information can be combined with best practice guidance available from other sources, including the online 'Service Management Body of Knowledge - SMBOK' (available through an annual subscription at http://www.smbok.com), and local conditions, to create standard operating procedures.

Later in this publication, the concept of a *'scenario action plan'* is introduced, to provide a means by which modifications to standard operating procedures can be minimized, and the dynamic aspects maintained separately in a scenario action plan catalog.

All service change management activities begin with 'initiate'.

The Initiate Activity

The 'INITIATE' activity represents the creation of a new change request record. It starts the lifecycle of every recorded change and begins the process of compiling change related information. The 'INITIATE' activity may also be the result of a review of reported information from past change request history, and the repeat of a previous change request. Anyone can initiate a change.

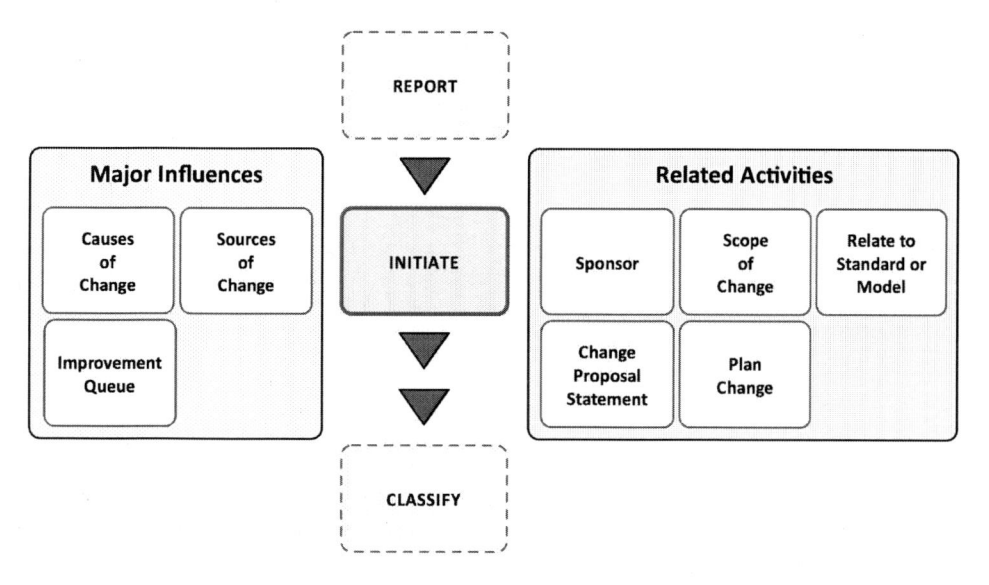

Figure 16: The Initiate Activity

Objectives

The objectives of the 'INITIATE' activity include:

- To ensure the service change management lifecycle is initiated appropriately;
- To initiate a change request event as close to the time of its need as possible;
- To document as much information and facts about, a change request to enable it to be effectively and efficiently processed through its lifecycle;
- To collect key sponsorship information and additional authorization for timely processing;
- To produce a concise record of supporting information;
- To collect information regarding the scope of the change, parties impacted, and likely resources required to implement;

- To collect and related information associated with any change proposal statement;
- To relate a change to a change model or standard change to accelerate the authorized response.
- To begin the process of formulating a change plan;
- To prepare all information required by the 'CLASSIFY' activity.

Type

The 'INITIATE' activity is typically a back-stage action but can be performed as a front-stage action in the case where a sponsor is requesting a change via service request received by the support function.

Key Inputs

There are a number of key inputs to the activity, including:

- Information provided by an improvement queue record;
- Information related to:
    - A change in business direction;
    - A new requirement for an existing service;
    - New or changed legislation;
    - Response to customer dissatisfaction with service;
    - Resolving a problem or incident;
    - Introduce new or upgraded service infrastructure (configuration item);
    - The application of maintenance;
- Information provided by output from the 'REPORT' activity, this may include:
    - The results of analysis performed by other service management practice areas;
    - Information reporting on previous change records;
- A service request:
    - To add a new service;
    - To add a new service subscriber;
    - To add new staff.

Major Influences

The major influences of this activity are:

- **Cause of change:** The availability of a list of common causes of change;
- **Sources of change:** The availability of a list of acceptable sources of change;
- **Improvement queue:** The current queue of approved improvements generated by a combination of a continuous improvement program and problem management.

Related Activities

The related sub-activities for this major activity include:

- **Sponsor:** This sub-activity ensures the information is collected regarding the sponsorship of a change request;
- **Scope of change:** This sub-activity collects information and states the scope of the change, including from an organization, location, and affected party perspective;
- **Relate to standard or model:** This sub-activity checks the change catalog to verify if the change can be matched to an existing change model, or standard change. If a match is found the change is related and cloned to accelerate progress through the remainder of the lifecycle by pre-population of information such as assignments, resource allocations, as defined by an authorized change plan. This sub-activity remains active until such time as it is known whether this change is a candidate for match;
- **Change proposal statement:** This sub-activity optionally prepares a change proposal statement in support of the request;
- **Plan change:** This sub-activity begins the process of formulating the change plan.

Actors:

This activity may involve actions by any of the following actors:

- A change sponsor;
- A change coordinator responsible for the change;
- A change agent;
- Any stakeholder role as a source of supporting information;
- Any service provider role, including specialists as a source of supporting information;
- Any third-party subject matter expert.

Key Outputs

There are a number of key outputs from the activity, including:

- Sufficient sponsorship and planning information to populate an change record and enable classification;
- A service change record.

The Classify Activity

A multi-level scheme is used to ensure the type of change is systematically classified and accurately described, enabling appropriate allocation of resources and response, effective assignment, and efficient processing. The classification scheme and 'CLASSIFY' activity relates the change to the affected release, stakeholder community, vital mission activity, service infrastructure component (configuration item), and service.

Correct classification of a change is the key to a timely response, suitable governance, the proper performance reporting of service levels, and ensuring the quality and efficiency of the practice and support process.

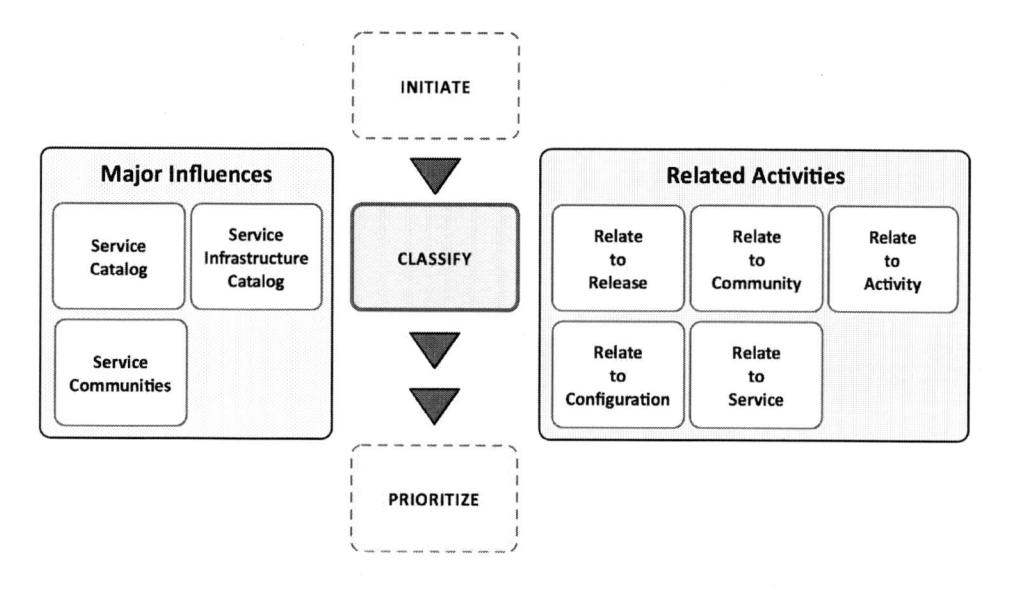

Figure 17: The Classify Activity

Objectives

The objectives of the 'CLASSIFY' activity include:

- To systematically classify a change and it's related information to ensure its correct routing and efficient processing through the support and change lifecycles;
- To relate a change to a release and specifically a release unit and package;
- To relate a change to affected and interested stakeholders communities;

- To relate a change to a vital mission activity, key objective or outcome, and enable proper assessment of true impact;
- To relate a change to a service infrastructure or configuration item;
- To relate a change to a service;
- To relate a change a situation level to assist prioritization;
- To relate the change to other pre-existing, known changes – the change constellation.

Type

The 'CLASSIFY' activity is typically a back-stage action.

Key Inputs

The key inputs to the 'CLASSIFY' activity, include:

- A change record that has successfully been processed and had its information properly formatted and populated by the 'INITIATE' activity.

Major Influences

The major influences of this activity are:

- **Service catalog:** The authorized list of services containing descriptions of their status, scope of operation, and functionality;
- **Service infrastructure catalog:** The list of the types of service infrastructure domains and items;
- **Service communities:** The information available about the communities served. This information may be contained within individual service contracts, or a summary of the customer communities using each service.

Related Activities

The related sub-activities for this major activity include:

- **Relate to release:** This sub-activity relates the change to an authorized release unit and package;
- **Relate to community:** This sub-activity identifies the 'parties of interest' relevant to the change scenario. The parties will include at least one stakeholder community, and any other community, group, role, or individual that has an interest in, or is directly affected by the change. This information is key to the 'ASSESS RISK' and 'APPROVE' activities, and in determining the actual scope of total impact of a change;

- **Relate to activity:** This sub-activity relates the incident record to a vital mission activity and an outcome, objective or key performance target resulting from completion of the activity;
- **Relate to configuration:** This sub-activity relates the change to the operation and current condition of a service infrastructure item, also termed a configuration item;
- **Relate to service:** This sub-activity relates the change record to an authorized service listed in the service catalog. The service does not necessarily need to be authorized for use via a service contract or agreement.

Actors:

This activity may involve actions by any of the following actors:

- A change coordinator responsible for the change;
- A change agent;
- Any service provider role, including specialists as a source of supporting information;
- Any third-party subject matter expert.

Key Outputs

The key outputs from the activity, include:

- A correctly classified change record.

The Prioritize Activity

The PRIORITIZE activity sets the relative importance of a service change when compared with other changes. The activity defines the order of importance and precedence of a change request, and mandates the commitment of resources and sequencing of work effort. The priority is used to determine the requested target time to complete the implementation, and is the basis for 'SCHEDULE' activity.

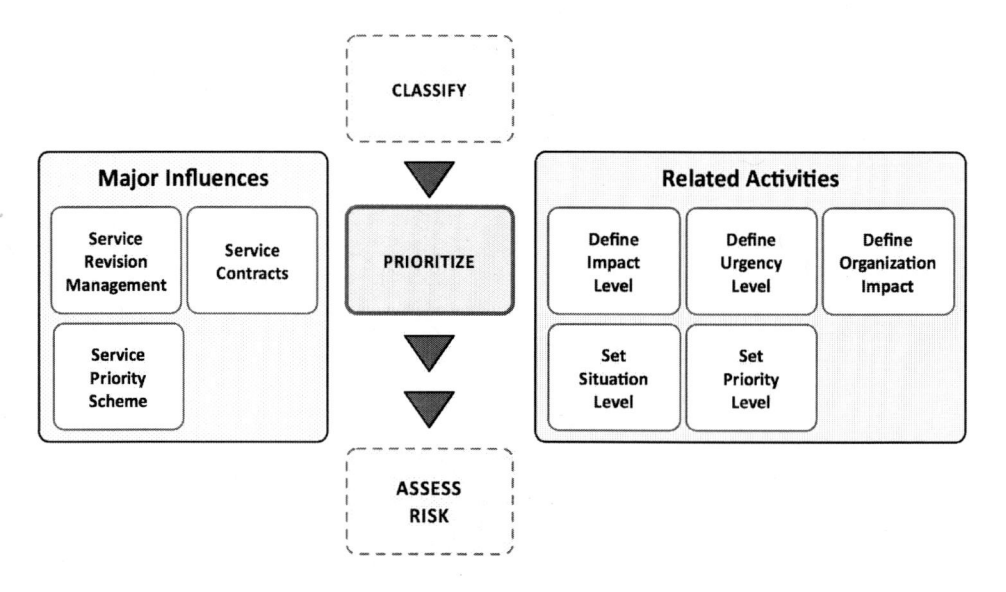

Figure 18: The Prioritize Activity

Objectives

The objectives of the 'PRIORITIZE' activity include:

- To ensure the priority of the change is properly set based the sponsor request and to set the requested priority level;
- To define the impact level provided by the sponsor to the change record;
- To define the urgency level provided by the sponsor to the change record;
- To define the organizational impact level provided by the sponsor to the change record;

- To set the situation level associated with the change, relative to the overall situation level within service provider operations. The situation level is used to ensure resource allocation and work effort is dedicated with consideration of external major events and critical situations, such as local disasters, weather conditions, and environmental parameters;
- To submit the fully formed change record, consisting of stated impact, urgency and organizational impact, and priority information, to the change queue.
- To sequence the work effort required to assess the risk of the change.

Type

The 'PRIORITIZE' activity is typically a back-stage action.

Key Inputs

The key inputs to the 'PRIORITIZE' activity, include:

- The current change record and its relationship with any other change records, projects, or constellations;
- A service contract relevant to the service, situation, customer, location, or activity being performed;
- The current change record information on stated impact and urgency;
- The service revision plan;
- The current situation level and noted situation conditions and projections;
- An opportunity statement from the improvement queue containing verified impact statements;
- A problem record containing verified impact statements;
- The service priority scheme for the specific service, customer, location, activity combination.

Major Influences

The major influences of this activity are:

- **Service revision plan:** The availability of the current relevant service revision plans;
- **Service contracts:** The contracts and individual guarantees they contain (also termed service level objectives), detailing the commitments of the service provider organization, and criteria for 'normal operations' and acceptable levels of quality of service;

- **Service priority scheme:** The formula referenced for determining the priority of a specific combination of service, customer, location and activity. The service priority scheme is generally based upon an agreed target time to restore normal service, with timing based upon earliest completion.

Related Activities

The related sub-activities for this major activity include:

- **Define impact level:** This sub-activity defines the stated impact to named stakeholders affected by the change, it also ensures the aggregate impact is described;
- **Define urgency level:** This sub-activity defines the stated urgency, or necessary speed to implement the change and restore normal service;
- **Define organization impact:** This sub-activity defines the stated impact to any affected organization or community and includes considerations such as their operational practices, culture and even reward systems;
- **Set situation level:** This sub-activity checks, sets or resets the situation level based upon the conditions of the incident;
- **Set priority level:** This sub-activity sets the priority level based upon terms established for use through the change management procedures. This is a change management term.

Actors:

This activity may involve actions by any of the following actors:

- A change sponsor;
- A change manager;
- A change coordinator responsible for the change.

Key Outputs

The key outputs from the activity, include:

- A service change record with a defined priority based upon change management terms, and a target time to complete the implementation.

The Assess Risk Activity

The 'ASSESS RISK' activity uses established risk management methods to assess the probability of risk resulting from threats to assets introduced by the change request. The activity also recommends countermeasures to eliminate or mitigate the risks to an acceptable and affordable level. The risk assessment scope includes financial, technical feasibility, organizational impact, and service degradation and interruption.

Risks when identified, and assessed as to their potential severity of loss and to the probability of occurrence, are assigned a relative 'risk priority number', and added to the 'Composite Risk Index'.

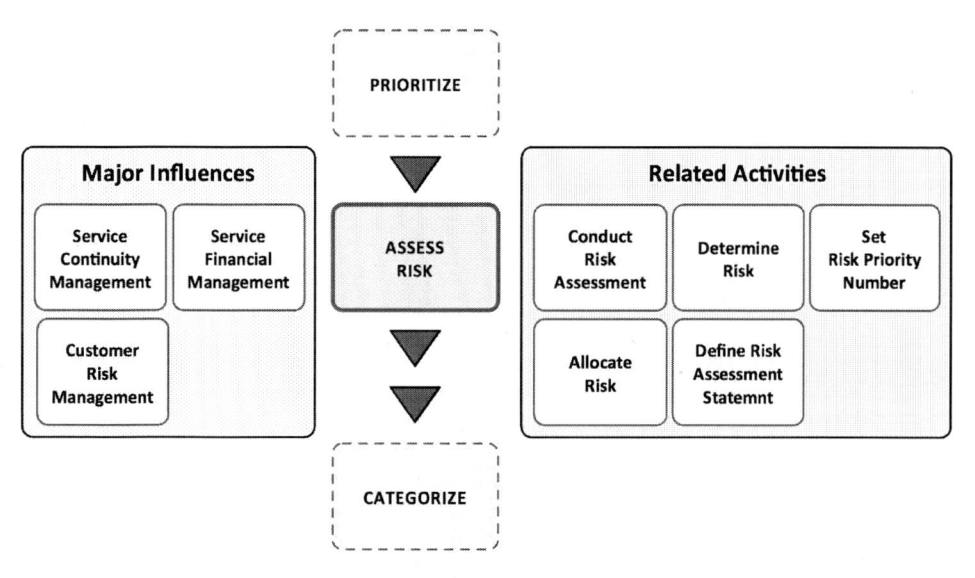

Figure 19: The Assess Risk Activity

Objectives

The objectives of the 'ASSESS' activity include:

- To coordinate a risk assessment of the change request;
- To determine and state the level and probability of risk;
- To set the relative risk priority number and add the risk statement to the composite risk index;

- To coordinate the definition of any necessary risk countermeasures to mitigate or eliminate the identified risks;
- To allocate (share) the risk and countermeasure actions amongst stakeholders;
- To define an aggregate risk assessment statement associated with the change request.

Type

The 'ASSESS' activity is typically a back-stage action involving inspection of policies and procedures. It may occasionally involve front-stage actions where the analysis requires the involvement of consumers, key stakeholders, sponsors and third parties.

Key Inputs

The key inputs to the 'ASSESS' activity, include:

- A prioritized change request.

Major Influences

The major influences of this activity are:

- **Service continuity management:** The availability of service continuity plans and service continuity planning and risk assessment skills;
- **Service financial management:** The availability of financial skills and methods to help determine the benefit statement and return on any investment;
- **Customer risk management:** The availability of customer risk management practices, methods and roles to provide a customer centric perspective and information.

Related Activities

The related sub-activities for this major activity include:

- **Conduct risk assessment:** This sub-activity distributes work orders to authorize the completion of risk assessments, and coordinates the their completion using organization-wide approved risk management practices;
- **Determine risk:** This sub-activity determines the risk, probability, impact, and likely countermeasures;
- **Set risk priority number:** This sub-activity sets the relative risk priority number;
- **Allocate risk:** This sub-activity allocates the known risk to the sponsor and stakeholders;
- **Define risk assessment statement:** This sub-activity defines a risk assessment statement for the change request and adds the statement to the composite risk index.

Actors:

This activity may involve actions by any of the following actors:

- A change sponsor;
- A change manager;
- A risk manager;
- A service customer (risk) manager;
- A change coordinator responsible for the change;
- Any role required to provide information to assist in the risk assessments.

Key Outputs

The key outputs from the activity, include:

- An risk assessed change request;
- One or more risk statements supported by completed risk assessment work orders;
- A record in the composite risk index.

The Categorize Activity

The 'CATEGORIZE' activity associates a governance framework and levels of authorization required by the 'APPROVE' activity as the final stage of the approval process. The level at which change is authorized is proportional to the identified level of risk, and or associated 'cost of change'.

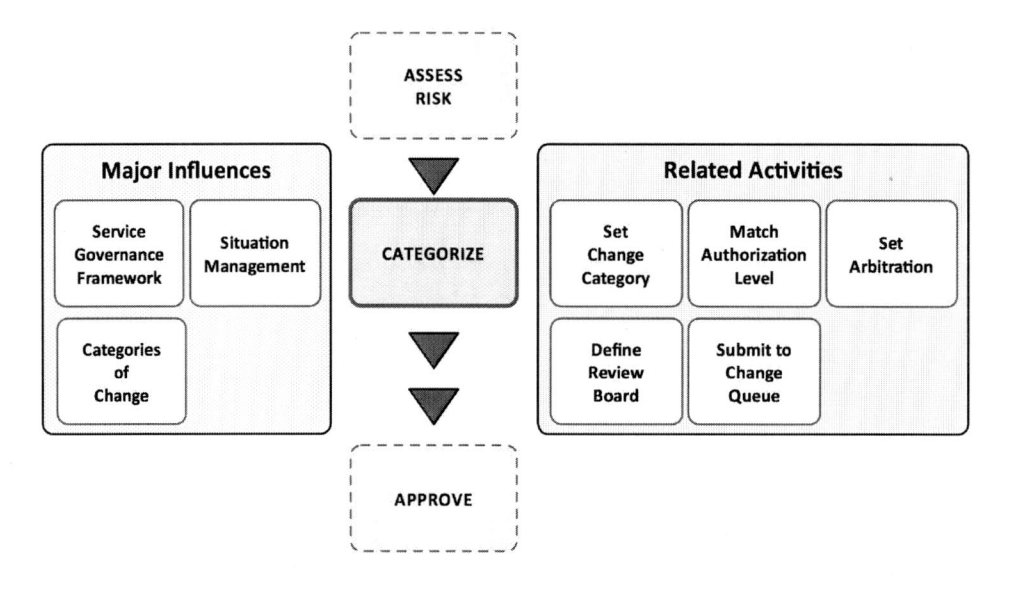

Figure 20: The Categorize Activity

Objectives

The objectives of the 'CATEGORIZE' activity include:

- To set the category for the change request;
- To match the approval authorization level with the change category;
- To relate and set arbitration and right of appeal procedures;
- To define the review board that will provide oversight of the approval, either the CRB, or CRB-HR;
- To submit the change request to the change queue for approval.

Type

The 'CATEGORIZE' activity is typically a back-stage action.

Key Inputs

The key inputs to the 'CATEGORIZE' activity, include:

- A risk assessed change request;
- The change categorization scheme;
- The change authorization levels;
- The arbitration procedures;
- The governance framework specific to the service involved.

Major Influences

The major influences of this activity are:

- **Service governance framework:** The availability of information on the policies, procedures and operational rules to manage changes to the specific service and service infrastructure targeted by the change request;
- **Situation management:** The availability of information on current and projected 'situations'. A situation is a condition or set of environmental parameters and major incident styled events that when they occur cause the service provider organization to radically adjust the documented and agreed service level guarantees, in favor of responding to the situation;
- **Categories of change:** The availability of the change categorization scheme describing the criteria for each category of change.

Related Activities

The related sub-activities for this major activity include:

- **Set change category:** This sub-activity assigns a category to the change;
- **Match authorization level:** This sub-activity matches and associates the change request with a predefined authorization level based upon the assigned change category;
- **Set arbitration:** This sub-activity relates and sets the arbitration and appeal procedures for the change request to be used should any party involved disagree with the category and authorization levels set;
- **Define review board:** This sub-activity defines which change review board will provide oversight and administration of the approval;
- **Submit to change queue:** This sub-activity submits the change request to the change queue and schedules it for final approval.

Actors:

This activity may involve actions by any of the following actors:

- A change manager;
- A change sponsor;
- A change coordinator responsible for the change.

Key Outputs

The key outputs from the activity, include:

- A categorized change request with an assigned change review board and set of arbitration procedures;
- An entry in the change queue and updated schedule for the approval process.

The Approve Activity

The 'APPROVE' activity provides 'final' approval for the change request to be resources, scheduled, and implemented as planned. The 'APPROVE' activity runs continuously alongside the 'RESOURCE', 'SCHEDULE', 'BUILD', 'TEST' major activities to support the continuation of the change through its lifecycle. It can also be invoked during the 'IMPLEMENTATION' activity to authorize actions required to remedy a failed change during implementation, or to reverse, or 'backout' a change.

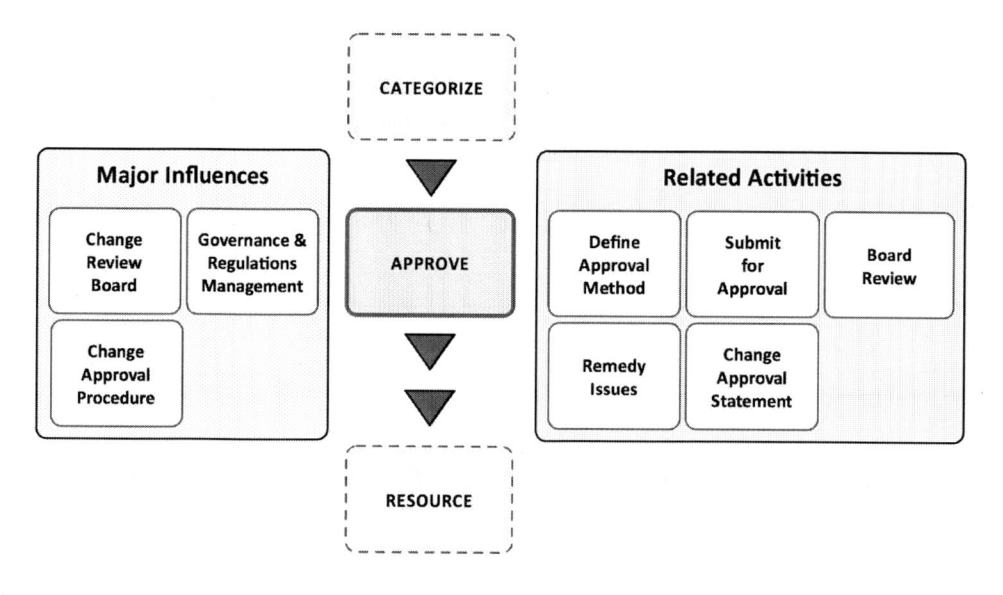

Figure 21: The Approve Activity

Objectives

The objectives of the 'APPROVE' activity include:

- To approve a change request for implementation;
- To define and agree the approval method and procedure;
- To submit the change request to a review board for approval;
- To complete a review by the assigned board;
- To document and remedy any issues identified by the review board;

- To define a change approval statement detailing the approval method used, observations made, decisions, issues identified with their impact, remedial actions, and subsequent approval procedures and criteria assigned for the remainder of the change lifecycle;
- To relate the approval statement to the change request and associated change plan.

Type

The 'APPROVAL' activity is typically a back-stage action performed within the confines of approval boards.

Key Inputs

The key inputs to the 'APPROVE' activity, include:

- A description of the approval methods;
- The governance framework specific to the service involved;
- A description of change review boards and organizational and operational structure;
- A description of arbitration procedures;
- A description of procedures to remedy issues identified during a review;
- A service contract relevant to the service, situation, customer, location, or activity being performed;
- The change plan;
- The change approval procedure.

Major Influences

The major influences of this activity are:

- **Change review board:** The availability of information describing the organizational design, key roles, policies, principles required to form and operate a change review board with authorization levels proportional to the category of change;
- **Governance and regulations management:** The availability of policies and procedures in the form of a governance framework to support decision making for service related changes. The information should respect and incorporate governance related to prevailing regulatory compliance at all levels, from enterprise to operational;

- **Change approval procedure:** The availability of documentation on the procedure followed by a review board to approve a change request.

Related Activities

The related sub-activities for this major activity include:

- **Define approval method:** This sub-activity defines and associates the approval method to be used to approve the change request;
- **Submit for approval:** This sub-activity submits the change request to the queue for approval by a review board;
- **Board review:** This sub-activity represents the review by a change review board of a change request, consisting of a combination of remote access and face-to-face meetings;
- **Remedy issues:** This sub-activity represents the documentation of issues with a change request, and the actions taken to mitigate or eliminate, remedy the issues;
- **Change approval statement:** This sub-activity creates a change approval statement, describing the extent to which, and conditions under which, a change request is, or is not approved.

Actors:

This activity may involve actions by any of the following actors:

- A change manager;
- A change sponsor;
- A change coordinator responsible for the change;
- A change review board member.

Key Outputs

The key outputs from the activity, include:

- An approved change request;
- A plan of remedial action;
- A change approval statement.

The Resource Activity

The 'RESOURCE' activity allocates resources to the work order activities required to implement a change request. The resources include human effort, hardware, software, and any assets required, internal and external to the organization. The activity includes determination of the planned effort involved, the required skills, and confirmation of the availability of the resources. This activity may be performed as part of the change review board procedures, and 'APPROVE' activity.

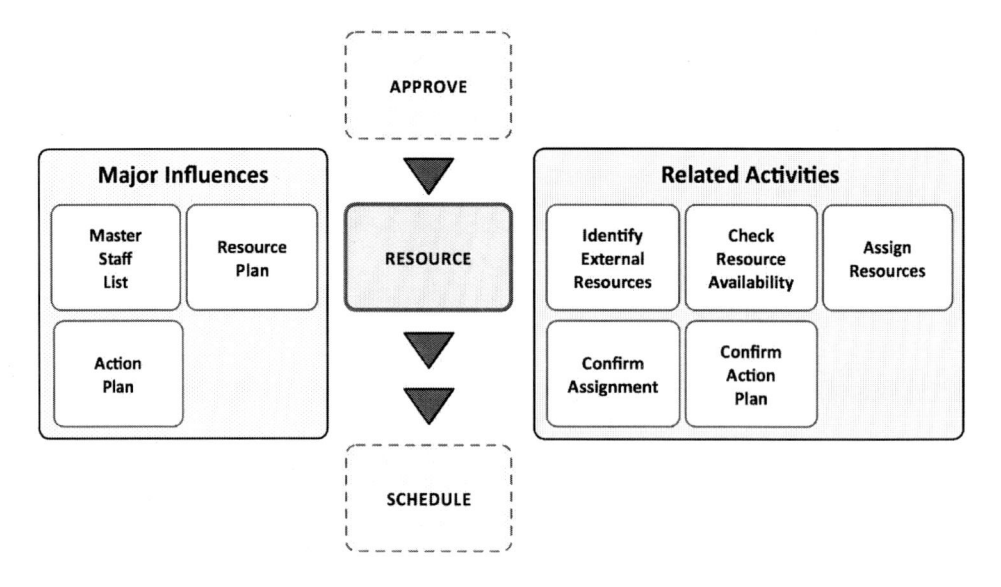

Figure 22: The Resource Activity

Objectives

The objectives of the 'RESOURCE' activity include:

- To ensure the change request work effort is fully resourced;
- To ensure any external resource requirements are identified and fulfilled;
- To ensure the availability of all resources is known and documented as part of the change record;
- To assign resources to the change request and related work orders;
- To confirm the assignment of resources with the resource or their supervisor;
- To confirm the action plan and change plan statements on resource requirements;

- To invoke and manage escalation routines to ensure resource needs are met, or to issue notifications for any exceptional circumstances, such as unavailability or insufficient capacity or capability.

Type

The 'RESOURCE' activity is typically a back-stage action that may invoke front-stage actions to identify the availability and capability of resources, and confirm assignments.

Key Inputs

The key inputs to the 'RESOURCE' activity, include:

- An approved change request;
- A service contract relevant to the service, situation, customer, location, or activity being performed;
- The master staff list describing roles, skills, knowledge and abilities;
- The governance framework with specific information on the role taxonomy and skills base;
- The authorized change plan and its associated resource and action plans;
- The related action plan and resource plan if part of a solution;
- The current workload effort across all service provider organization functional areas;
- The current situation level and noted situation conditions and projections.

Major Influences

The major influences of this activity are:

- **Master staff list:** The availability, accuracy and currency of the master staff list;
- **Resource Plan:** The availability, accuracy and currency of a resource plan;
- **Action plan:** The availability, accuracy and currency of an action plan.

Related Activities

The related sub-activities for this major activity include:

- **Identify external resources:** This sub-activity identifies the external resources, of all types, required to complete the planned actions;
- **Check resource availability:** This sub-activity checks the resource availability, and their stated capabilities and performance characteristics. This includes governance role, knowledge, skills and abilities with respect to people;
- **Assign resources:** This sub-activity formally assigns a resource to an action, either as part of the change plan, or a specific work order. The work order assignment is subject to modification and enhancement during the 'BUILD' activity;
- **Confirm assignment:** This sub-activity confirms the resource assignment, with the resource itself if possible, or with any supervisory or management responsibility. Confirmation is in documented form;
- **Confirm action plan:** This sub-activity confirms that all the resource requirements defined in the action (or change) plan are satisfied and documented as such. This activity also ensures a formal response is on record of the confirmation by the resource or person responsible for the resource.

Actors:

This activity may involve actions by any of the following actors:

- A change manager, to arbitrate as required;
- A change sponsor, to reinforce plan requirements;
- A change coordinator responsible for the change;
- Any stakeholder role as a source of supporting information;
- Any service provider role, including specialists who are a resource, or are contributing resources of any kind;
- Any third-party subject matter expert who is a resource, or are contributing resources of any kind.

Key Outputs

The key outputs from the activity, include:

- A resourced change request;
- A confirmed change resource plan;
- Documentation in support of resource assignments and acceptance;
- Statements as to resource issues or constraints, with likely impact and recommended course of action.

The Schedule Activity

The 'SCHEDULE' activity confirms the actual date and time the change will be implemented and completed. The activity restates the desired date based upon output from the 'RESOURCE' activity, and associates the change request and its work effort with an available change slot on the calendar of change events, known as the 'change schedule'. In doing so, the activity formally schedules the change and notifies all interested and involved parties of the timing. The scheduling is a result of comparing the priority, with the requested target time for completion of the change request, the resource availability, available change schedule slots, and arriving at an actual or scheduled target time. This activity may be performed as part of the change review board procedures, and 'APPROVE' activity.

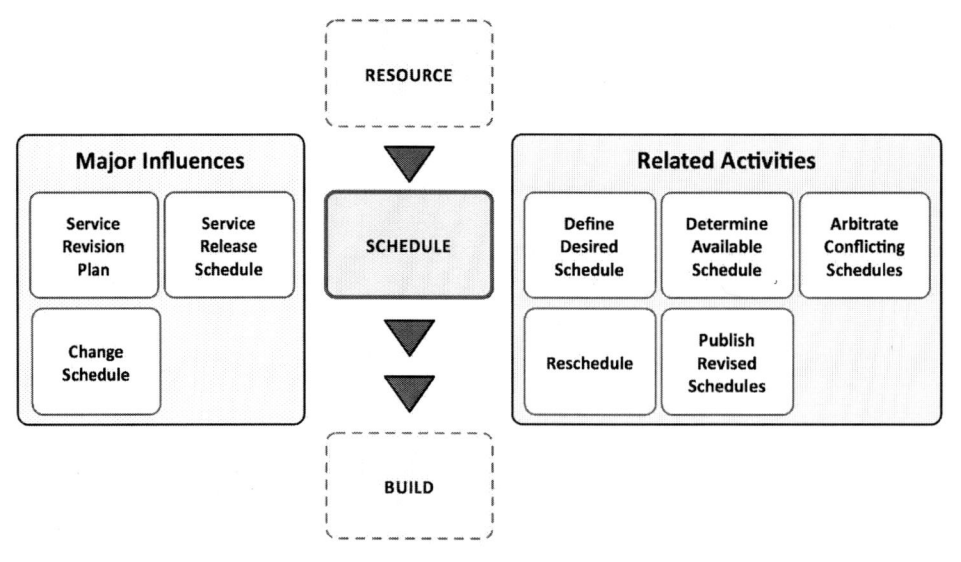

Figure 23: The Schedule Activity

Objectives

The objectives of the 'SCHEDULE' activity include:

- To set a planned target date and time for completing the implementation of the change request;
- To restate the desired schedule based upon confirmed resource assignments;
- To determine the available and suitable change schedule slots;

- To synchronize the target date with the service release and service revision plan schedules;
- To arbitrate conflicting schedules;
- To reschedule any item as a result of arbitration;
- To associate the target date with an available change slot in the change schedule;
- To publish the revised change schedule, providing information as necessary to support republication of any associated schedule, and issuing notifications to all interested parties.

Type

The 'SCHEDULE' activity is typically a back-stage action.

Key Inputs

The key inputs to the 'SCHEDULE' activity, include:

- An approved change request;
- The service revision plan, specifically key dates for planned revisions, and critical processing periods;
- The service release schedule, specifically dates and times when changes are allowed, and disallowed;
- The requested target date and time information contained in the change record as part of the change or action plan;
- The change release schedule;
- The arbitration procedure and policies for reconciling scheduling conflicts.

Major Influences

The major influences of this activity are:

- **Service revision plan:** The availability of a current plans describing the type, and timings of service revisions for any service affected by the change request;
- **Service release schedule:** The availability of the current service release schedule describing the release strategy for any service affected by the change request;
- **Change schedule:** The availability of a current change schedule.

Related Activities

The related sub-activities for this major activity include:

- **Define desired schedule:** This sub-activity restates and defines the desired and requested target time for implementing and completing the change request based upon new information output from the 'RESOURCE' activity;
- **Determine available schedule:** This sub-activity determines the availability of suitable change schedule slots and associates the change request and its work effort with an available change slot on the calendar of change events, in effect setting the planned target date and time for completing the implementation of the change request;
- **Arbitrate conflicting schedule:** This sub-activity arbitrates any scheduling conflicts and documents the issue, and recommended course of action;
- **Reschedule:** this sub-activity reschedules the change request as necessary should conflicts occur, and not be overcome. This may require a return to the 'APPROVE' and 'RESOURCE' major activities;
- **Publish revised schedule:** This sub-activity publishes the new change schedule with the addition of the change request, and notifies all interested parties of the availability of the new change schedule.

Actors:

This activity may involve actions by any of the following actors:

- A change manager, to arbitrate as required;
- A change sponsor, to confirm target schedule and optionally assist in any rescheduling;
- A change coordinator responsible for the change;
- Any stakeholder role as a source of supporting information;
- Any service provider role, including specialists who are responsible for a related or supporting schedule, such as facilities management, release management, and procurement;
- Any third-party who is responsible for a related schedule of any kind.

Key Outputs

The key outputs from the activity, include:

- A scheduled change request with an actual target date and time, and allocated change schedule slot;
- A revised change schedule;
- Documentation in support of the agreed target schedule;
- Statements as to schedule conflicts and issues, with likely impact and recommended course of action.

The Build Activity

The 'BUILD' activity prepares the formal work orders based upon the scheduled completion date, and assigned change slot in the change schedule. The 'BUILD' activity also prepares any special testing related work orders not already defined in the original action plan, as well as any actions required to stage, publish, install and conduct 'fit for purpose' or acceptance testing.

The activity includes the building of work orders required to define and operate a communications plan, controlling the dissemination of information about the progress of the change, as well as governance designed to perform release management actions and promote the change and associated resources to target environments.

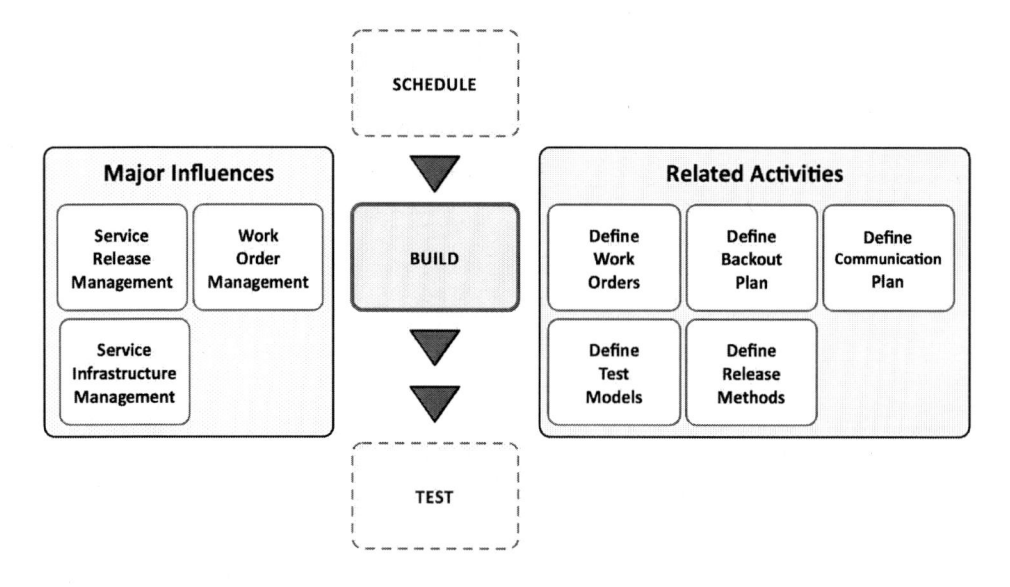

Figure 24: The Build Activity

Objectives

The objectives of the 'BUILD' activity include:

- To prepare all the work orders required to implement, complete, review and close the change request;

- To define a backout strategy and associated work orders, including any continuity related actions, which may be invoked to reverse the effect of the request;
- To define ca communications plan designed to ensure all interested parties and stakeholders are suitably informed via their preferred methods of the progress of the change request;
- To define work orders in support of the test plan spanning pre-implementation testing and post implementation acceptance testing, and review;
- To define work orders to support the release management methods and procedures.

Type

The 'BUILD' activity is typically a back-stage action.

Key Inputs

The key inputs to the 'BUILD' activity, include:

- Authorization to the perform the activity, in the form of a work order assignment;
- Documentation on existing control barriers;
- An approved change request;
- Work order creation, distribution and verification procedures;
- The authorized change plan and its associated resource and action plans;
- The related action plan and resource plan if part of a solution;
- A backout strategy and plan within the change plan;
- A communications plan within the change plan;
- A test plan within the change plan;
- Documentation on release management methods;

- The master staff list describing roles, skills, knowledge and abilities;
- The governance framework with specific information on the role taxonomy and skills base;
- The requested target date and time information contained in the change record as part of the change or action plan;
- A lexicon of terms and common language for the service infrastructure items.

Major Influences

The major influences of this activity are:

- **Service release management:** The availability of documentation on the strategy, policies and procedures to use to 'release' a service release;
- **Work order management:** The availability of documentation describing the protocols, policies and procedures for creating and distributing work order assignments;
- **Service infrastructure management:** The availability of key definitions of concepts and terms by service infrastructure management to describe the service infrastructure.

Related Activities

The related sub-activities for this major activity include:

- **Define work orders:** This sub-activity defines all the work orders required to progress the change request through the remainder of the change lifecycle. This includes work orders to authorize testing, the actual implementation, post implementation review, interviews to complete the change, and to close the change request after a successful review;
- **Define backout plan:** This sub-activity defines the backout plan based upon the strategy authorized in the change plan. The backout procedures will likely call upon established release management procedures used to implement the change;
- **Define communications plan:** This sub-activity defines the work orders required by the communications plan described and authorized by the change plan;

- **Define test models:** This sub-activity defines the testing routines required to both test the change prior to implementation, and to test from an acceptance perspective post implementation;
- **Define release methods:** This sub-activity defines the release management related work orders required to stage, distribute and install service infrastructure as required by the release plan.

Actors:

This activity may involve actions by any of the following actors:

- A change coordinator responsible for the change;
- The service release manager;
- The service infrastructure manager;
- A change sponsor, to confirm target schedule and optionally assist in any rescheduling;
- A change coordinator responsible for the change;
- Any stakeholder role as a source of supporting information;
- Any service provider role, including specialists who is skilled in, and has knowledge of, the procedures required to be defined to a work order;
- Any third-party who is skilled in, and has knowledge of, the procedures required to be defined to a work order.

Key Outputs

The key outputs from the activity, include:

- A cohesive set of detailed work orders, including dependencies, required to
- A backout plan;
- A communications plan;
- A test plan and test models;
- Documentation and information references to support the work orders.

The Test Activity

The 'TEST' activity represents all of the activities performed to conduct thorough pre-implementation testing of the actions required to make the change, and to prevent any degradation or impact to services, or waste of resources, resulting from a failure. The 'TEST' activity includes the actions required to document and resolve any test failures, describe the readiness to deploy, and to stage release packages, either to reverse the result of one or more work orders, or to promote elements of the change to the target environments. The 'TEST' activity includes all the testing activities, irrespective of whether they are performed by internal or external, third-party resources.

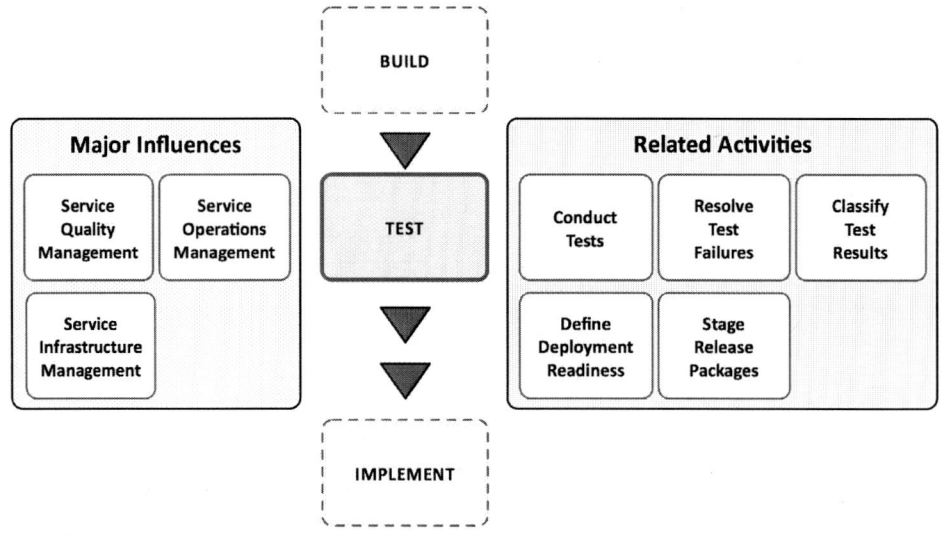

Figure 25: The Test Activity

Objectives

The objectives of the 'TEST' activity include:

- To test all aspects of the change request including performance, security, maintainability, supportability, reliability, availability, as well as functionality to ensure no failures occur either during the implementation, or as a result;

- To prepare a controlled test environment, and use quality management methods and criteria to rigorously conduct testing, and identify the extent to which testing can, and is performed;
- To establish a recovery point for the change and affected service infrastructure environment, representing the conditions to execute a backout or reversal if required;
- To ensure tests are conducted in an unbiased manner and by parties independent to key stakeholders;
- To prepare the service infrastructure environment for change by staging release packages.

Type

The 'TEST' activity is a back-stage action with occasional front-stage actions invoked as required to communicate progress to affected stakeholders and third parties.

Key Inputs

The key inputs to the 'TEST' activity, include:

- Recovery routines and procedures;
- A specification and description for the 'last known working configuration';
- Continuity plans and procedures;
- Authorization to the perform the activity, in the form of a work order assignment;
- Documentation on the test plans and units of testing;
- Documentation on the operational procedures;
- An approved change request;
- A test plan within the change plan;
- A backout strategy and plan within the change plan;
- A communications plan within the change plan;
- Documentation on release management methods;
- The master staff list describing roles, skills, knowledge and abilities;
- The governance framework with specific information on the role taxonomy and skills base.

Major Influences

The major influences of this activity are:

- **Service quality management:** The availability of testing methodologies and minimum test criteria, and test and performance management knowledge and skills from service quality management;
- **Service operations management:** The availability of information on the current operational policies, procedures, to start, restart, backup, and recover the service infrastructure component;
- **Service infrastructure management:** The availability of key definitions of concepts and terms by service infrastructure management to describe the service infrastructure.

Related Activities

The related sub-activities for this major activity include:

- **Conduct tests:** This sub-activity represents the completion of all the testing routines, scripts and procedures and the creation of the documentary evidence confirming testing has been completed, and the levels of success, and descriptions of failures and recommended courses of action;
- **Resolve test failures:** This sub-activity resolves any tests that failed, or seeks conditional permission to continue with the change implementation;
- **Classify test results:** This sub-activity classifies the test results following the resolution of any failed tests, and documents in detail the test results, including any conditional waivers, future remedies and countermeasures;
- **Define deployment readiness:** This sub-activity defines and documents the deployment readiness of the change and associated release package;
- **Stage release packages:** This sub-activity conditionally promotes or demotes the elements of the change request based upon the classified test results, and places the elements in predefined staging areas under the jurisdiction and management control of release management.

Actors:

This activity may involve actions by any of the following actors:

- A change coordinator responsible for the change;
- A change agent;
- Any stakeholder role as a source of supporting information;
- A service quality manager;
- The test manager;
- Any service provider role, including specialists as a source of supporting information;
- Any third-party subject matter expert;
- The service release manager.

Key Outputs

The key outputs from the activity, include:

- Staged release packages;
- A statement of deployment readiness;
- A completed and classified test plan;
- The results of a backout plan if invoked.

The Implement Activity

The 'IMPLEMENT' activity represents the actions performed to apply a change to the target service environment, report progress, commission and stabilize the results, and define the actual benefit realized and resources consumed. This is the final activity performed prior to the change being reviewed and completed. It can represent the application of a containment procedure, temporary bypass, quick fix, or 'workaround', but typically involves a permanent solution or change.

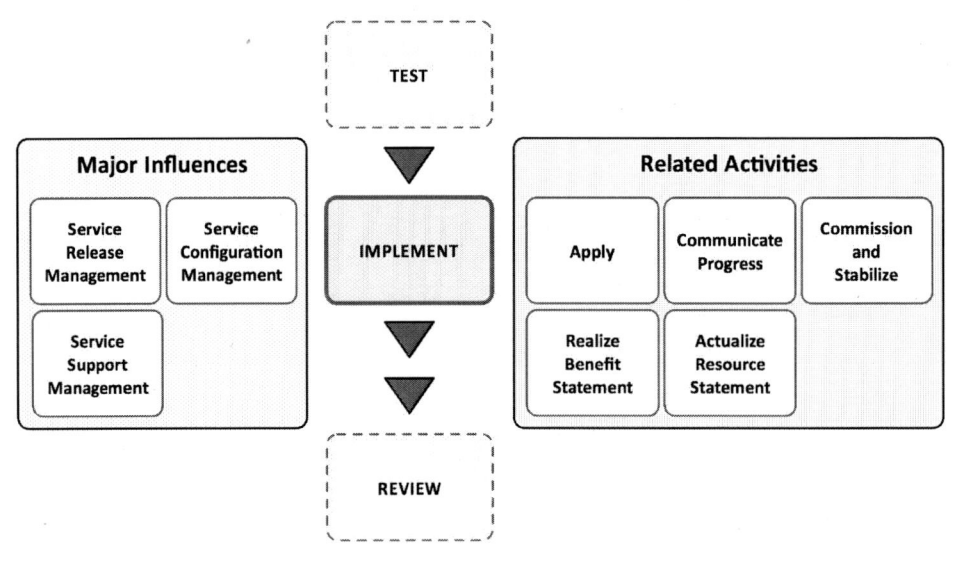

Figure 26: The Implement Activity

Objectives

The objectives of the 'IMPLEMENT' activity include:

- To successfully apply the change request to the target environment;
- To document and communicate progress regarding the implementation of the change;
- To monitor the success of the application of the change through a predefined 'warranty' or commission period, and ensure the effect of the change and its desired outcomes are stabilized;

- To determine and document the actual benefit realized as a result of applying the change;
- To determine and document the actual resources consumed to apply the change.

Type

The 'IMPLEMENT' activity is typically a back-stage action.

Key Inputs

The key inputs to the 'IMPLEMENT' activity, include:

- Authorization to the perform the activity, in the form of a work order assignment;
- Documentation on the operational procedures;
- Documentation on release management methods;
- Documentation on the target service configuration;
- A communications plan within the change plan;
- Documentation on the current service support procedures;
- Current benefit plan and statements contained within the change plan;
- Current resource plan and statements contained within the change plan;
- Documentation on the warranty/commission criteria;
- Documentation on the success criteria.

Major Influences

The major influences of this activity are:

- **Service release management:** The availability of documentation on the strategy, policies and procedures to use to 'release' a service release;
- **Service configuration management:** The availability of detailed information on the affected components, and their neighbors, within the service infrastructure, the service configuration;
- **Service support management:** The availability of information about the policies, procedures, current workload, and contact points and methods for service support.

Related Activities

The related sub-activities for this major activity include:

- **Apply:** This sub-activity represents all the actions to apply the change to the target environment;
- **Communicate progress:** This sub-activity represents the ongoing actions related to communicating progress information to interested parties and stakeholders about the status and condition of the change request;
- **Commission and stabilize:** This sub-activity performs all of the commission/warranty checks and verifies the success of the change as implemented. It ensures over a predefined period of time the change is stable and working as expected, and ensures the experiences are documented within the change history;
- **Realize benefit statement:** This sub-activity calculates the actual benefit realized as a result of implementing the change, offers a comparison with the projected benefit described in statements within the change plan, and obtains whatever fiduciary information and verification is required to substantiate the revised benefit statement;
- **Actualize resource statement:** This sub-activity calculates the actual and total resource consumption of the change request, and similarly offers a comparison with the projected resource usage described in statements within the change plan.

Actors:

This activity may involve actions by any of the following actors:

- A change manager;
- A change coordinator responsible for the change;
- Any stakeholder role as a source of supporting information;
- Any service provider role, including specialists as a source of supporting information;
- Any third-party subject matter expert.

Key Outputs

The key outputs from the activity, include:

- An implemented and applied change request;
- An updated benefit statement representing the benefit realized;
- An updated resource statement representing the actual resources consumed.

The Review Activity

The 'REVIEW' activity is performed by a change review board, or delegated and authorized authority that reports to the review board member. The 'REVIEW' activity inspects the activities performed throughout the entire lifecycle of a change request, and the results achieved of implementing the request, and verifies the desired results were achieved, and the associated work effort performed effectively and efficiently.

The 'REVIEW' activity, also known as a 'post implementation review', determines whether the change should be kept in place, or discarded. If discarded, either the backout procedures, or a continuity procedure is invoked to recover the last known working configuration and service environment.

The final action within this activity is to restore the service availability and enable access to its authorized customer communities.

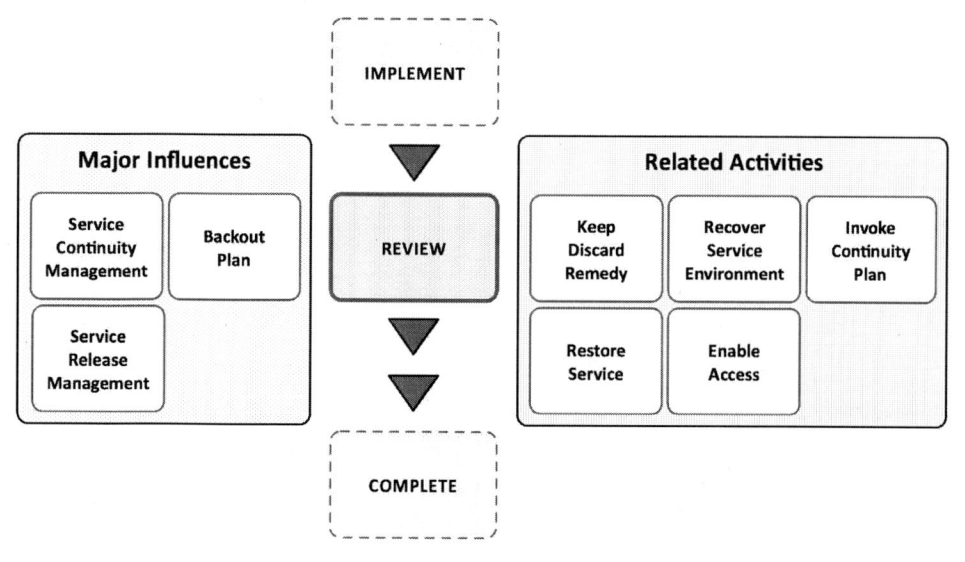

Figure 27: The Review Activity

Objectives

The objectives of the 'REVIEW' activity include:

- To review and report on the degree of success of the change request;
- To review and report on the effectiveness and efficiency of the activities performed in the change lifecycle in support of this request;

- To determine whether the change should be kept or discarded;
- To optionally recover and reinstate the previous service environment using the backout plan;
- To optionally invoke the continuity plan to recover the service environment;
- To restore the availability of the service;
- To enable access to the service.

Type

The REVIEW activity is typically a back-stage action.

Key Inputs

There are a number of key inputs to the 'REVIEW' activity, including:

- The complete change history record;
- Documentation on the work order activity;
- Any applicable change proposal statement;
- The change plan, including the original desired outcomes, action and resource plans, and test plans and results;
- The change approval statement;
- Documentation on the warranty/commission criteria.

Major Influences

The major influences of this activity are:

- **Service continuity management:** The availability of service continuity plan policies and procedures required to invoke a restoration of the service environment to an acceptable condition;
- **Backout plan:** The availability of the backout strategy and plan to invoke procedures to reverse the effect of the change request;
- **Service release management:** The availability of documentation on the strategy, policies and procedures to use to 'release' a service release, specifically the procedures to support a continuity plan or backout plan based reversal.

Related Activities

The related sub-activities for this major activity include:

- **Keep, discard, and remedy:** This sub-activity determines whether the chance has been successfully completed, has achieved the desired results, and should be kept. It also determines whether the change has failed and the change either discarded or remedied in situ;
- **Recover service environment:** This sub-activity optionally recovers the last known working configuration and service environment using the prescribed backout plan and procedures;
- **Invoke continuity plan:** This sub-activity optionally invokes the prescribed continuity plan procedures or countermeasures to return to the last known working service environment, or one that is at least acceptable;
- **Restore service:** This sub-activity restores the service availability;
- **Enable access:** This sub-activity enables authorized service communities to access the service and recommence normal operations.

Actors:

This activity may involve actions by any of the following actors:

- A change manager;
- A change sponsor;
- A change coordinator responsible for the change.

Key Outputs

There are a number of key outputs from the activity, including a service incident record:

- A post implementation review report;
- A remedy report of issues addressed in situ;
- A statement as to the circumstances and reasons for the invocation of the backout plan, and its results;
- A statement as to the circumstances and reasons for the invocation of a continuity plan, and its results;
- The change history record detailing timestamps for the entire lifecycle, including service restoration and service community enablement timings;
- A current, historical record of an existing service change.

The Complete (C1) Activity

The 'COMPLETE' activity is the first stage of closing a service change record. It represents a confirmation by service change management that all activities related to the implementation, and/or backout of a change request are successfully completed. Once a change reaches this stage, all activity except for standard communications with the stakeholder ceases.

This is a useful interim status, as it allows the support organization to complete the change record for reporting purposes and avoid having to perhaps coerce the customer into agreeing to a closure when they remain unsure about the success of a change.

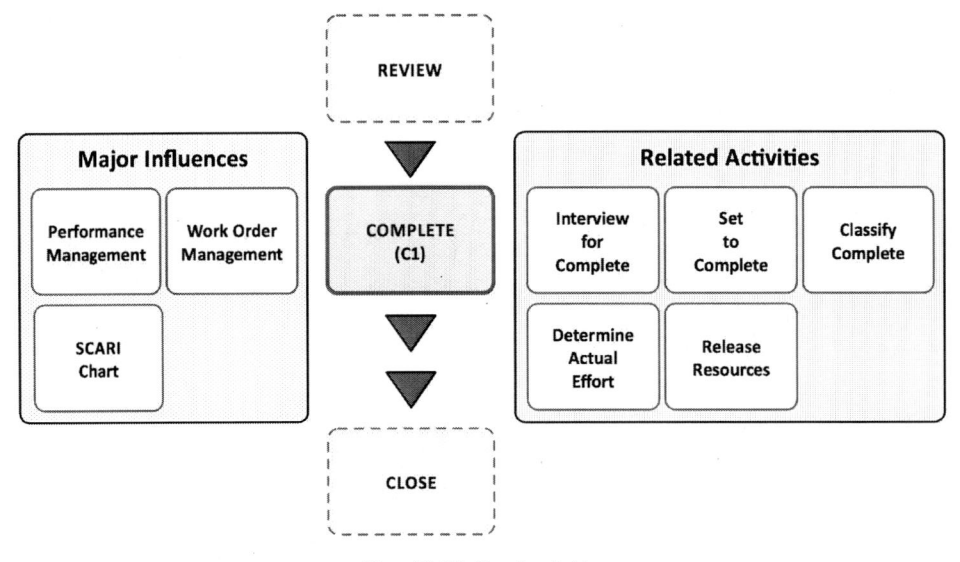

Figure 28: The Complete Activity

Objectives

The objectives of the 'COMPLETE (C1)' activity include:

- To interview all parties involved in a service change and confirm all related activity has been completed and further assignments can cease;
- To determine the actual effort involved in service change, including the post implementation review activity;

- To provide a documented checkpoint for all resource performance management reporting;
- To authorize the decommission and release of resources committed to the service change request.

Type

The 'COMPLETE' activity is typically a back-stage action.

Key Inputs

The key inputs to the 'COMPLETE' activity, include:

- The change plan, specifically the action and resource plans detailing the work performed;
- Complete change request records, including work order assignments and completion reports;
- Documentation on all post implementation work order related activity;
- Key performance measures from the prevailing performance management framework;
- Documented confirmation within the service change record of a successful implementation, and/or invocation of a backout or continuity plan, based upon the output from the 'interview to complete' sub-activity.

Major Influences

The major influences of this activity are:

- **Performance management:** The availability of performance related criteria to use to create the necessary checkpoints and supporting documents to report the work effort involved in the service change;
- **Work order management:** The availability of automated (or manual) systems, procedures and operational capabilities designed to assist in the scheduling and completion of work order effort;
- **SCARI chart:** Typically contained within an authorized change plan, checklists or simplistic diagrams describing the roles and their level of responsibility for a specific service change request. The SCARI chart is based upon the 'support, consult, accountable, responsible, and informed' governance criteria.

Related Activities

The related sub-activities for this major activity include:

- **Interview for complete:** This sub-activity verifies with each entity involved in the change request that all required response related activity has been completed successfully;
- **Set to complete:** This sub-activity sets all work order requests, and the overall service change status, to 'complete', and by doing so officially signifies change activity has ceased. This action provides a vital checkpoint for resource management and performance reporting;
- **Classify complete:** This sub-activity classifies the actions performed to complete the change, including the results achieved and level of success;
- **Determine actual effort:** This sub-activity confirms all work order related documentation is complete and describes the amount and duration of effort involved in the response. It also determines the actual effort of the response;
- **Release resources:** This sub-activity authorizes the decommissioning of resources committed to the change, and reallocation to other work efforts.

Actors:

This activity may involve actions by any of the following actors:

- A change coordinator responsible for the change.

Key Outputs

The key outputs from the activity, include:

- Documented authorization to cease all change related activity;
- Documentation to enable the determination of the total turnaround time or duration of the change request;
- Documentation to enable the determination the total work effort involved in the change request.

The Close (C2) Activity

The 'CLOSE' activity represents a confirmation by the sponsor and all stakeholder communities affected by change request of a satisfactory implementation of the change and restoration of normal service. It is the final stage of the change lifecycle.

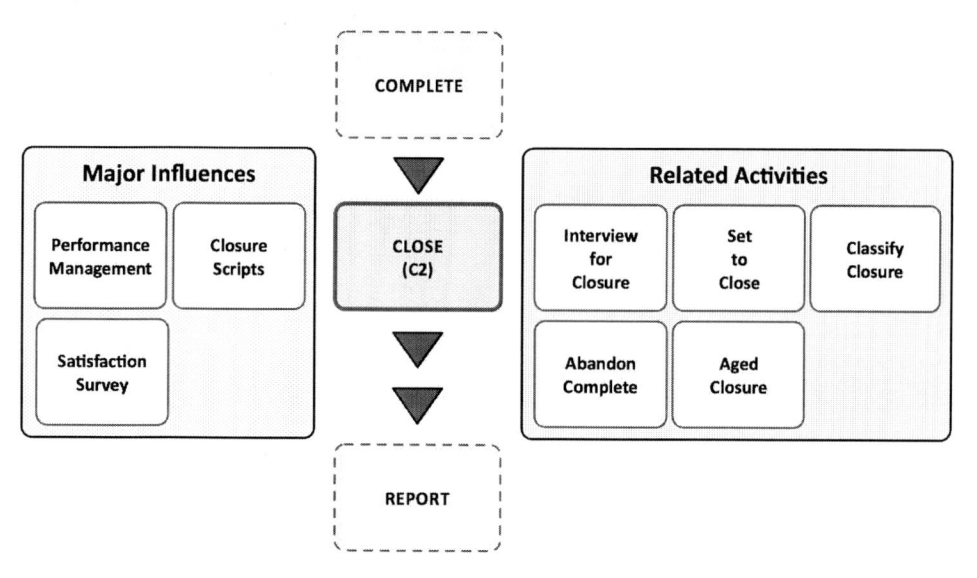

Figure 29: The Close Activity

Objectives

The objectives of the 'CLOSE' activity include:

- To interview all stakeholders impacted by a service change and confirm their satisfaction with the change, and restoration of service;
- To close the change history record;
- To close the opportunity history record;
- To optionally enable closure of a problem history record;
- To enable an optional, aged closure of the change record based upon a failure to contact one or more affected stakeholders;
- To provide a documented checkpoint for all resource performance management reporting.

Type

The 'CLOSE' activity is typically a front-stage action involving direct contact with the affected stakeholders under sensitive conditions to determine levels of satisfaction.

Key Inputs

The key inputs to the 'CLOSE' activity, include:

- Documented confirmation of the completion of a service change record;
- Documented confirmation of a stable solution via commission report;
- Approved satisfaction survey;
- Approved closure interview scripts;
- Key performance measures from the prevailing performance management framework;
- The governance framework with specific information on the role taxonomy and skills base.

Major Influences

The major influences of this activity are:

- **Performance management:** The availability of performance related criteria to use to create the necessary checkpoints and supporting documents to report the work effort involved in the service change implementation;
- **Closure scripts:** The availability of documentation on the interview process and interactions required to solicit confirmation of change closure from the sponsor and affected stakeholder communities;
- **Satisfaction survey:** The availability of approved satisfaction survey documentation and guidance on usage as part of, or subsequent to, the 'interview for closure' sub-activity.

Related Activities

The related sub-activities for this major activity include:

- **Interview for closure:** This sub-activity verifies with each stakeholder community affected by the change of their satisfaction with the response and solution;

- **Set to close:** This sub-activity sets the status of the service change record and all associated work order requests to 'closed', and by doing so officially signifies a satisfactory response. This action provides a vital checkpoint for resource management and performance reporting;
- **Classify closure:** This sub-activity classifies the change record based upon the conditions under which the change was closed. For example, it may have been conditionally closed, or some work orders may have been incomplete but found unnecessary;
- **Abandon complete:** This sub-activity is invoked when one or more stakeholders offer an unsatisfactory response. The sub-activity amends the classification and status of the change to 'incomplete', and causes the escalation and notification routines to alert all involved of the response;
- **Aged closure:** This sub-activity is optionally invoked when stakeholders are unable to be contacted to conduct the 'interview for closure' sub-activity. It enables 'ageing', and allows for closure of a change record after a specific period of time has elapsed without the occurrence of a related service incident. Its use requires specific authorization by the change manager, and is governed by specially documented conditions.

Actors:

This activity may involve actions by any of the following actors:

- A change manager, only the change manager can authorize the closure of a service change request;
- A change sponsor;
- A change coordinator responsible for the change;

Key Outputs

The key outputs from the activity, include:

- Documented authorization from the affected stakeholders the change record may be closed;
- A closed service change and completed history record;
- Documentation to enable abandonment of the previous complete status.

The Report Activity

The 'REPORT' activity is performed at specifically timed intervals to generate information in the form of standard sets of reports for use by service management, service support, and service change management responsibilities, to assist in making decisions regarding service level attainment. The reports are also used to measure and manage the effectiveness and efficiency of the service provider organization's change related operations.

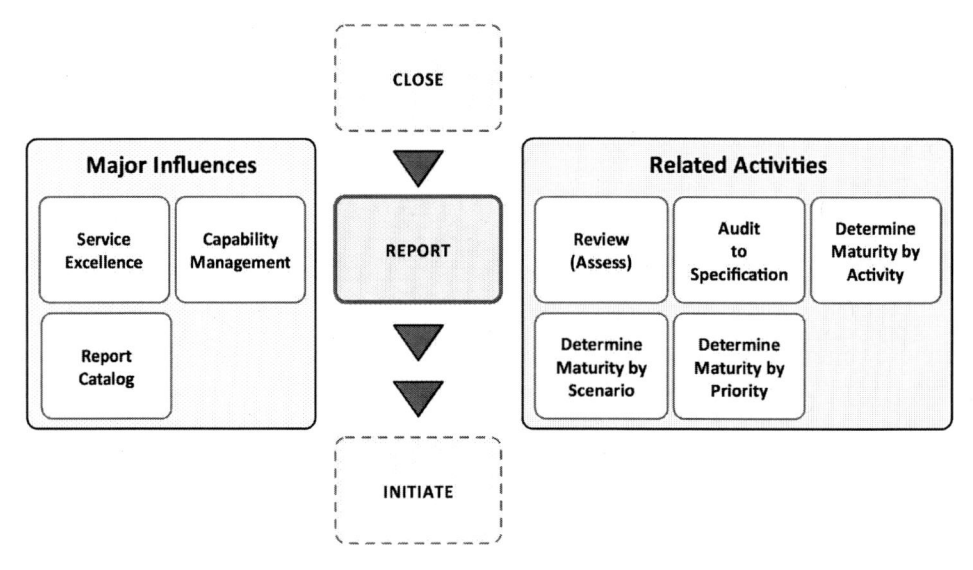

Figure 30: The Report Activity

Objectives

The objectives of the 'REPORT' activity include:

- To enable a review or internal assessment of the effectiveness and efficiency of the service change procedures, and authorized change plans;
- To enable an audit or inspection by an unbiased third-party with no interest in the outcome of the appropriateness of the service change procedures, and authorized change plans;
- To report on all change-related activity and history;
- To assist in the determination of the level of the maturity of the change plan by vital mission activity;

- To assist in the determination of the level of the maturity of change practice for each specific change situation;
- To assist in the determination of the level of the maturity of the change practice by the assigned priority of the change.

Type

The 'REPORT' activity is typically a back-stage action.

Key Inputs

The key inputs to the 'REPORT' activity, include:

- Change management database and change record history;
- Performance criteria for an assessment;
- Compliance criteria for an audit;
- Maturity level criteria;
- A service contract relevant to the service, situation, customer, location, or activity being performed;
- The governance framework specific to the service involved;
- Any associated problem and solution plan records;
- Any associated change constellation records;
- The opportunity statement;
- The service priority scheme for the specific service, customer, location, activity combination.
- Documentation on the work order activity;
- Any applicable change proposal statement;
- The change plan, including the original desired outcomes, action and resource plans, and test plans and results;
- The change approval statement;
- Documentation on the warranty/commission criteria.

Major Influences

The major influences of this activity are:

- **Service excellence:** The availability of criteria to support a service excellence based assessment of operations;
- **Capability management:** The availability of criteria to support a maturity level based assessment of operations;
- **Report catalog:** The availability of detailed specifications for required reports, including their purpose, required content, intended message, target audience, and publishing format and schedule.

Related Activities

The related sub-activities for this major activity include:

- **Review (assess):** This sub-activity assists in the assessment of the effectiveness, appropriateness, and efficiency of the change procedures and change plan, and in general the service change management practices;
- **Audit to specification:** This sub-activity assists in readying the organization and information audit trail to support the audit of the compliance or conformance of service change management practices to specified criteria;
- **Determine maturity by activity:** This sub-activity assists in the determination of the level of the maturity of the service change management practices by vital mission activity affected;
- **Determine maturity by scenario:** This sub-activity assists in the determination of the level of the maturity of the service change management practices for each specific change request situation;
- **Determine maturity by priority:** This sub-activity assists in the determination of the level of the maturity of the service change management practices by the assigned priority of the change.

Actors:

This activity may performed by any of the following actors:

- A change manager;
- A change sponsor;
- A change coordinator responsible for the change;
- A change agent;
- Any stakeholder role as a source of supporting information;
- Any service provider role, including specialists as a source of supporting information;
- Any third-party subject matter expert.

Key Outputs

The key outputs from the activity, include:

- A report catalog of practice related reports;
- Various change related reports designed to meet the need of their specific audiences;
- An assessment report;
- An audit report;
- A maturity level statement or report.

This page is left intentionally blank.

Key Performance Measures

Introduction

The following guidance represents measures that can be arranged into common groupings, and can additionally be related to each of the major activities to provide a comprehensive performance management framework for the practice.

In general, measures should be established to provide visibility of the duration and effort required to complete each major activity, the time each between one activity completing and the next starting, and the total elapsed time to journey from the first activity to the last.

Quantitative (Frequency and Volume)

Quantative measures are based on quantity, frequency, volume, thresholds, throughput or a target number, and generally help measure levels of efficiency, rather than effectiveness or quality. The following measures should all include the total number within a time period, and where appropriate a percentage comparison, for example the percentage of changes that were successful, compared with those that were not:

- Changes by source;
- Changes resulting from one or more incidents;
- Changes by location;
- Changes by stakeholder group;
- Changes by vital mission activity;
- Changes by service or service family grouping;
- Changes by line of business;
- Changes by third-party agreement;
- Changes by priority of vital mission activity;
- Changes by classification;
- Changes incorrectly classified;
- Changes at each stage of the lifecycle;

- Changes by priority;
- Changes by common change area;
- Changes by type;
- Changes by category;
- Changes by impact;
- Change queue depth and width;
- Improvement queue depth and width;
- Change queue versus improvement queue.

Qualitative

Qualitative measures provide visibility and management control of an attribute or classification related to the effectiveness of an operation or activity, its quality. Occasionally expressed as a percentage comparison of actual versus expected, they tend to lack the numerical or statistical analysis found in a quantative measure. These types of measures often involve 'averages' or mean value over a time period.

The following measures tend to be in the form of a list, often of exceptions, but should all include a percentage based or comparative measurement where possible:

- The percentage of Changes closed satisfactorily, unsatisfactorily with reason;
- Changes completed using a workaround, by type of workaround;
- Changes closed using a change, by type of change (i.e. urgent);
- Changes currently opened without a scheduled workaround or change ;
- Changes expected to close next period by scheduled workaround or change;
- Changes caused by a workaround;
- Changes resulting from a service request
- Changes resulting from a change request;
- Changes requiring a change in the agreed priority;
- Average turnaround time for Changes by classification, service, and customer;
- Average age a Change remains in a 'complete' stage prior to closure, by type, customer, service, and Vital Mission Activity (VMA);
- Average turnaround time of Changes by priority;
- Changes incorrectly classified;
- Changes incorrectly prioritized;
- Changes matched to previous Changes;
- Changes matched to known errors;

- Changes matched to workaround;
- Changes matched to scheduled changes;
- Percentage of Changes correctly and incorrectly assigned;
- Percentage of Changes correctly and incorrectly classified;
- Percentage of Changes correctly and incorrectly completed/closed;
- Average age of a completed Change by priority, customer, service;
- Number of Changes bypassing the support desk;
- Number of Changes recorded 'after the fact';
- Instances where an Change was escalated;
- Number of Changes reopened after closure.

Financial

- Total cost of change, by type, service, priority, and scenario;
- Total cost of change management;
- Total cost of change management by location, customer, service;
- Total cost of backed out or abandoned changes;
- Total cost of incorrectly implemented or incomplete changes.

All of these measures are candidates for inclusion in service change report catalog items.

This page left intentionally blank.

Governance

Introduction

What is governance? Governance is the system by which the operations of an organization are directed and controlled. At the heart of a governance system are policies and rules to properly perform specific actions.

A governance structure or 'framework', also specifies the distribution of rights and responsibilities among different participants and stakeholders. It provides the rules and procedures for making decisions.

The USMBOK description of a governance framework discusses how governance spans actions and decisions made by the corporation or enterprise, the service provider organization, and within day-to-day operations, such as service change management.

A governance framework also includes the policies, procedures required to change elements of the framework, and incorporates specific compliance, such as that mandated by regulatory bodies. Also included is an arbitration process to manage situations where conflicts occur.

Although alignment of objectives and activities across an enterprise is a worthy product of a governance framework, it is not a primary goal. It is rather the result of good governance. Governance is more focused on articulating the division of responsibilities among different supervisory, regulatory, and enforcement authorities, and in doing so detailing any allocated any risks.

It assures decisions are made within the prevailing legal and ethical limits, the views of minorities are taken into account, and that the voices of all those affected by a decision are heard in decision-making. It is also responsive to the present and future needs of the organization.

Governance requires the formal definition of roles involved in decision-making as well as the careful listing of all the decisions falling within its scope under normal operations. Governance should also consider scenarios where exceptional circumstance alter the make up of roles and responsibilities, such as experienced during disaster recovery events.

The Scenario Action Plan Approach

This guide provides both an ideal starting point to develop a set of operational procedures, sometimes termed 'standard operating procedures or SOP', and a means of assessing the completeness of existing procedures.

The development of any procedures will require careful consideration of any governance. The governance will need to address creation, maintenance, and use of the policies and procedures for service problem management. It should also provide special guidance on the change control of procedural documentation.

Although the procedures fall under the jurisdiction of the service change management group, specifically the Change Manager, they are subject to approval by whoever is responsible for promising and agreeing to levels of service support.

The Problem with Policies and Procedures

It is often the case that as soon as a policy or procedure is documented, it is subject to change. This is especially so with problem related procedures. There are always opportunities to improve a support response with new diagnostic routines, resolution activities, and leveraging of new knowledge.

It is seldom an organization can create and maintain a version of a standard operating procedure (SOP) designed to meet the specific needs of all clients and all situations. Soon, SOPs become redundant and not referenced by the very support staff they are designed to help. This causes SOPs to become outdated almost as soon as they are developed, and introduce an unacceptable burden and cost with respect to their ongoing maintenance.

One way to protect against, or at least limit, the need to constantly change procedural documentation, is to separate the information that varies, from that which does not. The USMBOK guidance achieves through use of the 'scenario action plan (SAP)' concept.

The Scenario Action Plan (SAP)

A change can be related to any type of service request. A 'scenario action plan (SAP)' is a detailed description of the full context of a response to a service request developed from the provider's perspective, and used to document the actions authorized in a service provider response.

The SAP details the actions to be performed in response to a specific consumer scenario (see earlier description of this term), their sequence, as well as the roles involved and their level of responsibility. It also includes timings, key interactions, and estimates of the authorized work effort.

The SAP concept is designed to insulate standard operating procedures from the day-to-day dynamics of conducting service provider support, by maintaining situation specific information separate from the procedures.

Through its relationship with a consumer scenario, the SAP details the origin of the request, related vital mission activities and their key performance targets, environmental context, organizational context, and specific expectations (or needs depending on the existence of a service level agreement) surrounding the request. It also describes how a standard operating procedure is used to respond to the request.

This approach dramatically reduces the need for change, causing most, if not all change to be applied to the individual SAPs.

A catalog of SAPs can be maintained by the provider organization, and it is in the SAP documentation most change is made to reflect the changing needs of the client, and any adjustments in a response by the service provider.

The SAP can also act as a checklist or other visual aid intended to provide detailed guidance on the exact steps to completing a major activity, sub-activity, or task related to a specific situation or consumer scenario. This documentation also serves as training aid to teach individuals how to complete specific capacity related tasks.

In a service experience map, the SAP binds support processes to the provider and consumer pathways (see the following discussion on the service request pathway).

Service Request Pathway

Each service request has a *'pathway'* through the service management system. The service request or service pathway describes the authorized, programmed path of a service request through the service organization. Sometimes termed the 'workflow', the pathway also incorporates suitable governance, control barriers, performance measures, automated actions, escalation and notification routines as to ensure timely completion of all tasks or work orders associated to the pathway.

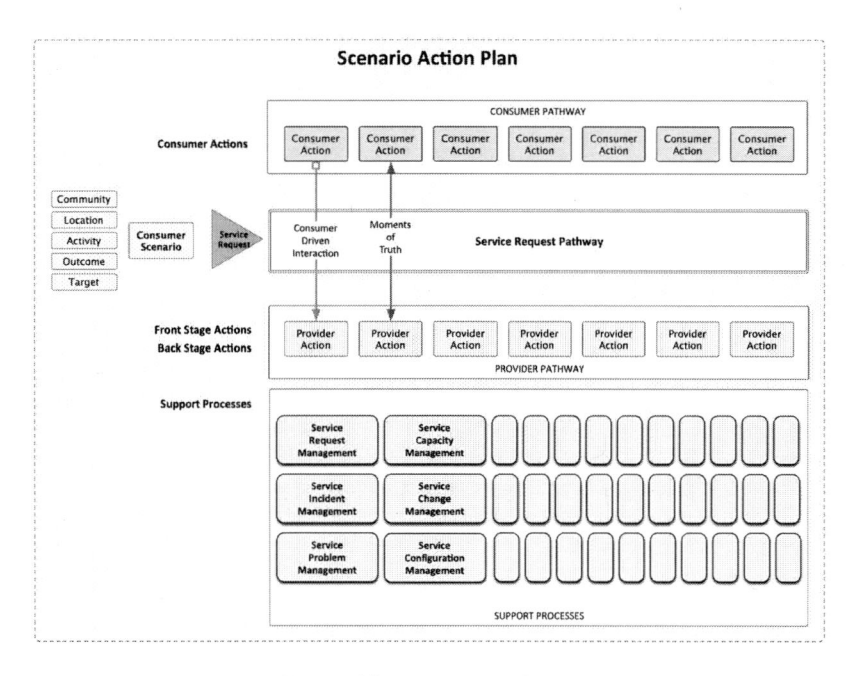

Figure 31: The Scenario Action Plan

The *'service request pathway'* is analogous to the clinical and patient pathways used in the healthcare service industry to define the activities and responsibilities of both the healthcare organization and the patient for specific situations. The definition of pathways is a critical element of any governance framework, and the management of the work along a pathway vital to finding and eliminating waste, and continuous improvement of operations.

A service request pathway is a combined description of the actions, interactions, communications, expectations and experiences of the consumer or customer (*'consumer pathway'*), and the provider (the *'provider pathway'*). The service request pathway is a major element of the *'service encounter'*.

A service request pathway is combined with the specific information about how support processes engage and operate under certain circumstances (as defined in a scenario action plan) and included as key documentation within the Configuration Plan described earlier in this publication.

When used, the scenario action plan and service request pathway concepts are key constituent elements of the Change Plan described earlier in this guide.

Mapping Practitioner Guide Roles to Client Roles

Another key element of defending against the need to constantly change standard operating procedures, is the use of industry accepted, 'best practice' based names for the key roles and responsibilities.

The following taxonomy of roles contained within this guide, can be mapped to roles described within an organizational chart as part of developing a set of custom standard operating procedures.

Practitioner Role	Client Equivalent Role
Service Customer Manager	
Service Fulfillment Manager	
Service Planning Manager	
Service Quality Manager	
Service Delivery Manager	
Change Sponsor	
Change Manager	
Change Coordinator	
Change Agent	
Support Specialist/Analyst	
Service Operations Manager	
Service Support Manager	
Service Infrastructure Manager	
Service Value Manager	

The SCARI Concept and Method

For a standard operating procedure to be truly effective, it's important to associate roles with the activities described, and when doing so make it clear what the level of responsibility is for that role, related to an action. The description of role involvement is not limited to just activities, and should include the creation of any information, artifacts, or inputs in general that either influence or direct an activity.

The term 'RACI' is a popular acronym used to describe a method for presenting the relationship between roles and activities in a diagram format. The acronym represents before traditional levels of responsibility: Responsible, Accountable, Consulted, and Informed.

This method is extended into the USMBOK, to include a fifth character 'S' representing 'supportive' and resulting in the term 'SCARI'. The SCARI term represents the following levels of responsibility:

- **S - Supportive:** Indicating the role is supportive, perhaps providing resources, knowledge, or skills to help complete an activity, or make a decision. As supportive the role does not perform an actual activity to complete the action or directly help to achieve the outcome. A supportive role can include sponsors and key stakeholders;
- **C - Consulted:** Indicating the role is consultative, and the role has information, knowledge, or know-how necessary to complete the activity;
- **R - Responsible:** Indicating the role is responsible for completing one or more actions required to complete the major activity or related activity;
- **A - Accountable:** Indicating the role is accountable for the activity being completed successfully, and achieving the desired outcome. Only one role can be assigned this level of responsibility for any major activity, related sub-activity, or major influence element;
- **I - Informed:** the role requires to be 'informed' as to specific progress, or must be notified of results, but need not be consulted. This is the most passive role and often represents that of a consumer, or executive level management.

In its simplest form of use, the SCARI method cross-references each role involved in an activity with the activity, and uses one of the letters mentioned to indicate the level of involvement or responsibility in the activity. The method provides important documentation of roles and responsibilities and can be quickly applied to any aspect of a standard operating procedure.

The SCARI Chart

Only one role may be made accountable for each activity. The activities can be described in a simple list form, and not necessarily in the sequence they are performed. A brief description should be described for each SCARI chart, and the most effective format is that of a question. For example:

"Three new sales agents are being added to the southeast sales organization, located in the regional sales office. These positions are additional to the current workforce.

The service level agreement has been updated and the extra demand authorized by service planning. Who is involved, and what is the level of their involvement, in the initial service capacity management activity of creating a capacity request to begin the process of providing these staff with the infrastructure they need to perform their duties?"

SCARI CHART

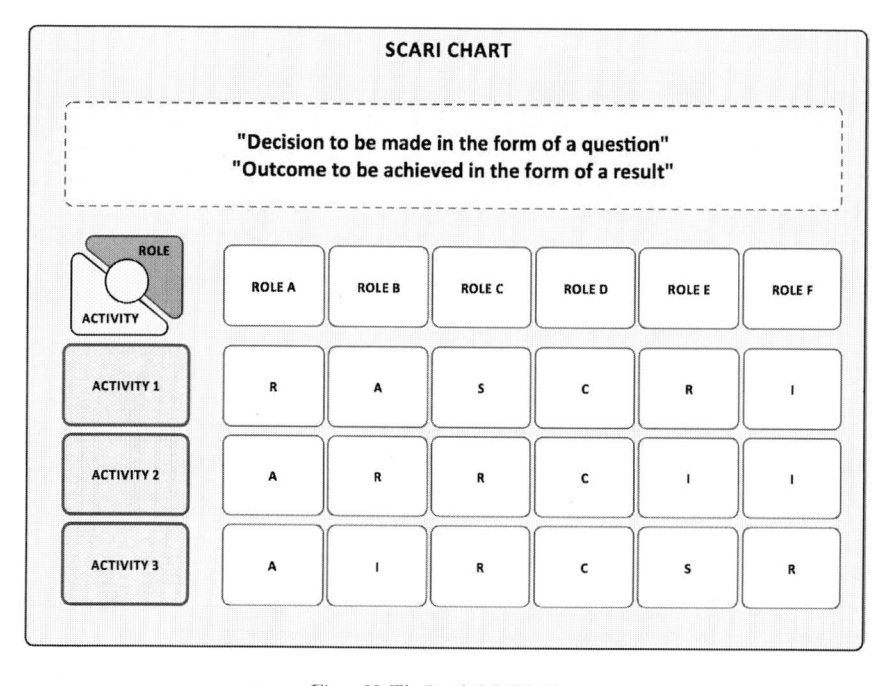

"Decision to be made in the form of a question"
"Outcome to be achieved in the form of a result"

ROLE / ACTIVITY	ROLE A	ROLE B	ROLE C	ROLE D	ROLE E	ROLE F
ACTIVITY 1	R	A	S	C	R	I
ACTIVITY 2	A	R	R	C	I	I
ACTIVITY 3	A	I	R	C	S	R

Figure 32: The Simple SCARI Chart

The SCARI chart can be attached to a brief explanation of the decision as well as a description of an activity.

For example:

"The current capacity management practices limit the amount approved under a normal capacity request for infrastructure to $5000. The infrastructure required by the new sales staff at the Southeast region averages $15,000 per employee. Who is involved, and what is their level of involvement, in the approval process for the purchase of this infrastructure given the amounts involved?

The previous diagram illustrates a SCARI chart in its simplest form, with activities listed in the left-hand column, cross-referenced with roles listed in the top role.

There is no limit to the number of activities or roles in a chart, whatever is practical or makes sense. These charts provide a useful check as to the understanding within a service provider organization of who is involved in performing the procedure and at what level of responsibility.

The Major Activity Template

Each major activity is described with up to three major influences, and five related (sub) activities.

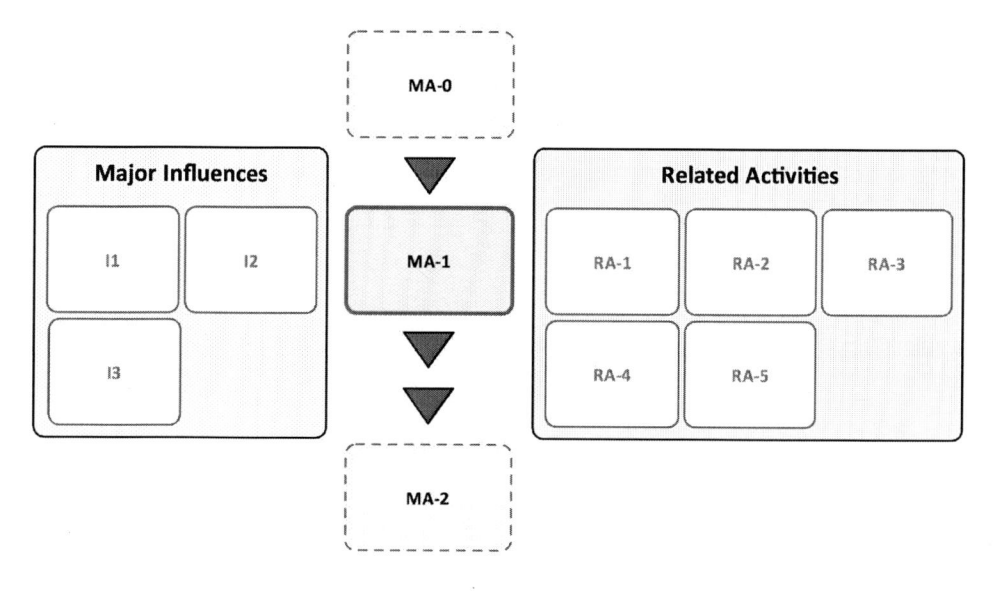

Figure 33: The Major Activity Template

A major activity diagrams contain the following elements:

- **Major Influences (I1, I2, I3):** Representing other knowledge domains, knowledge areas within a domain, or specific artifacts with a significant influence over the activity in the form of a key input, policy statements, or perhaps procedural integration or interoperation. In all cases these are three that are highlighted and favored, they do not represent a complete list;
- **Major Activities (MA-1):** Each major activity is described, including its objectives, key inputs and outputs, and actors;
- **Related Activities (RA1 through RA-5):** Five significant related activities, also termed sub-activities, are described for each major activity, providing comprehensive guidance on the work effort involved in completing the major activity. Similar to the major influences, these represent the more common or significant, and not a complete list of sub-activities.

Also described are the immediately prior major activity, and the next activity to be performed. In the diagram MA-0 represents the previous major activity, or last one performed, and MA-2 the next.

Combining Major Activity and SCARI Charts

Together, a combination of the role taxonomy (describing the names assigned to roles described in the SOP), SCARI designations (indicating the level of responsibility), and major activity diagram for any stage of a SOP, can provide substantial detail on how individual actions within a procedure, or the entire procedure is performed.

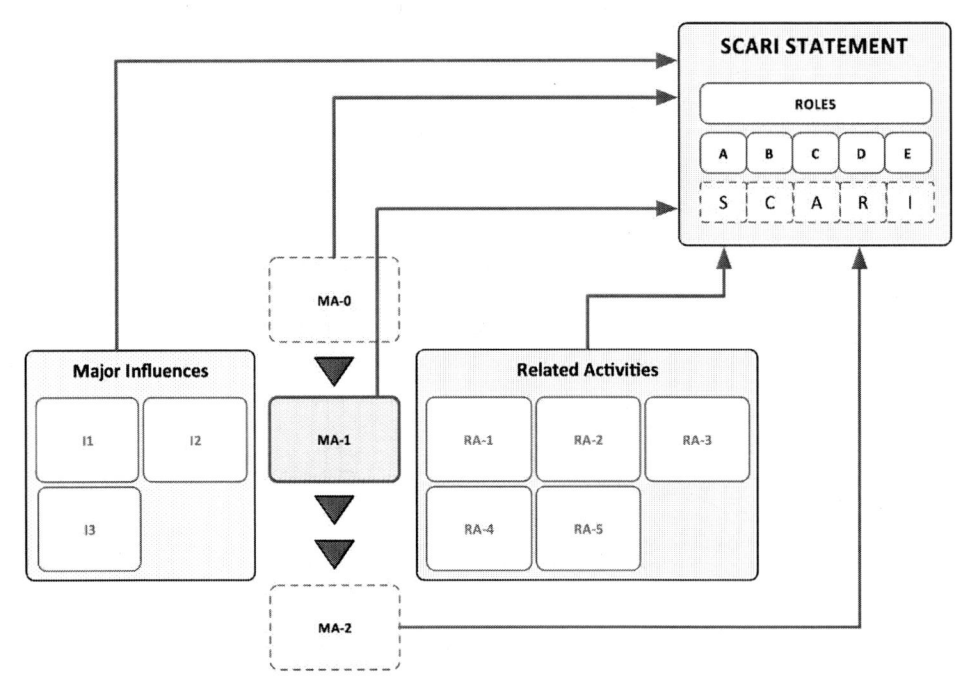

Figure 34: Mapping SCARI Roles to Major Activities

In the above diagram, which may seem complicated at first glance, each element of a major activity diagram can be associated with a SCARI chart and statement. This level of detail provides a better understanding of who might be involved in creating an artifact or policy that represents a major influence over a major activity, or similarly who is accountable for a key input, generated as an output from a previous major activity.

The method can be used to further document how to complete a major activity by providing a SCARI chart for each related (sub) activity. All SCARI charts and statements associated with a standard operating procedure are governed by change management policies and procedures.

Service Management 101 Services

Service Management Body of Knowledge™ (SMBOK)

An Internet subscription service providing access to thousands of best practice statements related to the provision of services, and specifications for a service management system and service provider organization.

URL: http://www.smbok.com

Service Management University™

An online learning system providing affordable access to the latest service management related education and topical information.

URL: http://www.sm101-university.com

Outside-In Service Management™

A program of onsite workshops designed to help apply outside-in (customer centric) thinking methods to manage the provision of services.

URL: http://www.smbok.com/pages/programs-home

Lean Service Management™

A program of onsite workshops designed to help apply lean thinking methods to manage the provision of services.

URL: http:// www.smbok.com/pages/programs-home

Virtual Service Manager™

An online support service provided on a complimentary best-effort basis to service management professionals. Customized support plans are available where a guaranteed response time is necessary.

URL: http://sm101-support.com

This page left intentionally blank.

INDEX

ADKAR Cycle 12
Approval 23
Backout Plan 22, 53
Back-Stage 35
Cause of Change 21
CFIA 69
Change
    Pre-Approved 58
    Proposal 51
    Proposal Statement 21
Change Agent 43
Change Catalog 59
Change Constellation 52
Change Coordinator 40
Change Equation 64
Change History 53
Change Lifecycle 65
Change Management
    Roles 36
    What is? 13
Change Management Group 46
Change Manager 38
Change Model 21, 58
Change Plan 22, 51
Change Queue 53, 59
Change Record 20
Change Review Board 47
Change Review Board/High Risk ... 48
Change Schedule 53, 60
Change Slot 53, 60, 71
Change Sponsor 37
Common Characteristics 3
Communications Plan 22
Consumer Scenario 20, 51
Continuity Plan 23

Continuity Response Team 49
Continuous Improvement 27
Continuous Improvement Cycle ... 27
Contracts and Vendors 45
Correlation 23
Cost of Change 71
Customer Pathway 140
Escalation 22
Essential Requirements 5
FMEA 52
Front-Stage 35
Goals and Objectives 17
Governance 137, 138
Impact 22, 52
Improvement Queue 21, 51
Inputs 73
Key Performance Measures
    Qualitative 134
Key Performance Measures
    Financial 135
    Qualitative 134
    Quantative 133
Major Activities 77
    Approve 97
    Assess Risk 91
    Build 108
    Categorize 94
    Classify 85
    Close 125
    Combining with SCARI Chart ... 146
    Complete 122
    Implement 116
    Initiate 81
    Intepreting Diagrams 80
    Phases 78

Prioritize	88	Roles	36
Report	128	Mapping	141
Resource	100	SCARI	
Review	119	Combining with Major Activity	146
Schedule	104	Concept	142
Template	145	SCARI Chart	61, 143
Test	112	Scenario Action Plan	26, 80, 138, 139
Major Influences		Scope	21, 26
Intepreting	80	Statement	20
Template	145	Security Incident	23
Model Change	21, 58	Service	22
No Fault	22	Legal Definition	15
Outputs	75	Service Change	51
Plain Language	24	Report Catalog	62
Post Implementation Review	23	Service Change Record	56
Principles	19	Service Encounter	140
Priority	53	Service Pathway	140
Problem Management	27	Service Request Pathway	140
Problem-Change Lifecycle	68	Service Support Role Taxonomy	35
Problems Managing	6	Situation	23
Related Activities		Solution Plan	23
Intepreting	80	Source of Change	7, 21
Template	145	Sponsorship	21
Relaters	20	Stakeholder Interest	22, 52
Relationship with		Standard Change	58
Configuration Management	33	Stewardship	21
Continuous Improvement	27	Success Factors	10
Incident Management	28	Support Processes	35
Problem Management	28	Support Specialist	44
Project Management	30	Test	23
Release Management	31	Test Plan	53
Release	53	Transfer of Command	23
Release Cycle	31	Transition State	2
Report Catalog	62	Type	9
Resource Management	25	Adaptive	9
Resources	25	Corrective	9
Risk Assessment	22, 52	Perfective	9
Risk Priority Number	52	Preventative	9

Project 20	Urgency 22, 52
Proposal Statement 21	Vital Mission Activity 51
Unified Command 24	Work Order 53, 60
Unique Identifier 57	Zone of Risk 33, 69